A Brief History of the Economy

Daniel Cohen

A Brief History of
the Economy

Preface by Esther Duflo

Translated by David Broder

polity

Originally published in French as *Une brève histoire de l'économie* © Editions Albin Michel – Paris 2024

This English translation © Polity Press, 2026

Polity Press
65 Bridge Street
Cambridge CB2 1UR, UK

Polity Press
111 River Street
Hoboken, NJ 07030, USA

ISBN-13: 978-1-5095-6830-7 – hardback

A catalogue record for this book is available from the British Library.

Library of Congress Control Number: 2025938383

Typeset in 11 on 14 pt Sabon LT Pro by
Cheshire Typesetting Ltd, Cuddington, Cheshire
Printed and bound in Great Britain by CPI Group (UK) Ltd, Croydon

The publisher has used its best endeavours to ensure that the URLs for external websites referred to in this book are correct and active at the time of going to press. However, the publisher has no responsibility for the websites and can make no guarantee that a site will remain live or that the content is or will remain appropriate.

Every effort has been made to trace all copyright holders, but if any have been overlooked the publisher will be pleased to include any necessary credits in any subsequent reprint or edition.

For further information on Polity, visit our website: politybooks.com

Contents

'How often have I watched, and longed to imitate when I should be free to live as I chose, a rower who had shipped his oars and lay flat on his back in the bottom of his boat, letting it drift with the current, seeing nothing but the sky gliding slowly by above him, his face aglow with a foretaste of happiness and peace!'

Marcel Proust, *Swann's Way*

Preface

by Esther Duflo, Nobel Prize in Economic Sciences

Daniel Cohen passed away on 20 August 2023, at the age of seventy.

It is at the age of seventy – as he tells us in the final chapter of this book – that we return to a thirty-year-old's level of happiness. He further tells us that we sometimes achieve the creativity that Beethoven enjoyed at the end of his life when, finally freed from the obligation to please others, he exploded the norms and the musical codes of the day. Indeed, it was then that Beethoven composed his five late sonatas (opp. 101, 106, 109–11),[1] a 'twilight' music of exceptional originality and brilliance. Unfortunately, Daniel Cohen did not have time either to enjoy the happiness of this age, or to treat us to a work from the twilight of his life.

The book in your hands makes me think more of another end-of-life work, the *Mass in B minor* by Johann Sebastian Bach. Completed a year before the

---

[1] I'd strongly recommend Igor Levit's rendition (published by Sony) – remarkably, his first album.

composer's death, the *Mass in B minor* is a masterful work, largely assembled from pieces composed throughout his career. It is often considered the enshrinement of a whole life, a synthesis of all Bach's stylistic and technical contributions, as well as being a profound spiritual reflection. For the neophyte, the *Mass in B minor* is an unforgettable introduction to Bach's choral music. For those who have been weaned on Bach, it is a refuge, a musical site where they can rediscover, like old friends, the essential moments of his work.

Similarly, this book takes up themes that ran throughout Daniel Cohen's work. Unlike the *Mass in B minor*, which is so long that it is rarely performed in its entirety, this is a concise work. In about a hundred pages, it takes up the essential themes that run through his work and his thinking: that of the suffering that comes from soaring growth, that of the tension between a limited world and an infinite desire, of globalization, the decline of civilizations, the tensions of the digital age, meaning and the pursuit of happiness. We also find familiar characters here: Marcel Proust, Jared Diamond, Richard Easterlin, Jean Fourastié, Leonard Cohen, Milan Kundera, and also Barbie . . .

All this is told in Daniel's unique voice. He submitted the manuscript in January 2023, a few weeks before a sudden illness forced him to be hospitalized, and he did not have the opportunity to revise it. If there is any glimmer of luck for us in this misfortune, it is this raw manuscript. For what we lose in 'polishing', we gain in immediacy. Even in the written text we perceive the modulations of tone, the passages in high notes, the animation of the hands, and Daniel Cohen's characteristic brilliance.

Preface

In the section in Chapter 7, 'Homo numericus', I was especially moved by the sentence: 'The idea that we can resurrect the dead by tapping into their "history" is utterly terrifying and entirely credible.' The passage refers to an episode of the TV series *Black Mirror* in which a young woman uses a (fictional, anticipatory) version of ChatGPT to bring back to life her husband who had died in a car accident, using his text messages, emails and writings to predict what he would have said in all and any situations. In this book, Daniel has given us the gift of his – wholly natural – intelligence. He leaves us something of himself by offering us a condensed version of his work, in a little nugget. There is surely nothing terrifying about this. Still, for his many friends and students it will be difficult to read this book without a certain sadness: he is so present in these pages that more than one person will yearn for the chance to go to lunch with him to talk about it.

For those who are new to Daniel Cohen, this book will offer them an overview of his thinking, a guided tour highlighting the important milestones, which they can explore in more depth by reading each of his previous books. I really discovered economics by reading (in one night in my dorm room at the brand new humanities faculty) the manuscript of *The Misfortunes of Prosperity*. Reading it changed my life, by opening me up to the richness of the discipline when it is practised, as it should be, as one among the human sciences. Let's bet that this book will have the same effect on young aspiring thinkers, whether they dream of becoming economists, historians, philosophers or politicians.

Although this is a posthumous work, it was never intended as a testament. At the time he was writing it, Daniel was full of life and plans, an early retiree from the École normale and the new president of the École d'économie de Paris, the institution that he had helped to found, thereby contributing to a profound transformation of the study of economics in Paris. He wanted to understand the world we live in, with its divisions and its tensions, the better to change it.

So, like the *Mass in B minor*, this book is more than an anthology of a career. Applied to a new context (the full Catholic Mass for Bach, the post-COVID world for Cohen), the lessons of built-up experience produce new perspectives.

What demands this new perspective is a certain anxiety, which dominates the last part of the book, before the concluding pages. There is no shortage of sources of concern. 'I'm worried about China', writes Daniel, quoting Proust's Madame de Guermantes. The management of the COVID-19 crisis in China, which banked on a zero-COVID policy at the expense of economic activity, accelerated a transition that was undoubtedly inevitable: China's demographic decline, extreme levels of saving and economic dependence on global demand were bound to cause growth to taper off, in a slowdown similar to that experienced by France at the end of the Trente Glorieuses (the so-called Thirty Glorious Years after 1945). But the difference is that, in China, the implicit contract between the regime and the population after Tiananmen was 'growth in exchange for (no) democracy'. As growth slows down, the political equilibrium is broken. 'China is still a cause for concern.'

Artificial intelligence, as we have seen, is 'utterly terrifying'. However, what 'makes the blood run cold'
for Daniel is not the idea that robots could one day be
as (or more) intelligent than us, but dehumanization
– the prospect of going to a supermarket and not meeting anyone there. There is a deeper logic driving this
dehumanization: for as long as services to people are
performed by humans (whether they be doctors, bank
or insurance employees, judges or waiters), productivity
growth bumps up against the limits of the human being.
If machines can replace humans, it becomes possible
again, in principle, to increase productivity infinitely by
honing the machines. For companies, there is an irresist-
ible temptation to enter this race. But by losing human
relationships, we lose the *raison d'être* of our activities,
and undoubtedly our own *raison d'être*. A robot with
the softest skin will never be able to replace the kindness
of a nurse taking care of an elderly person.

Climate change is a new source of possible disaster.
Here again, unlike most authors addressing this subject,
Daniel does not dwell on the physical description of the
problem or on identifying its possible technical solutions. Rather, he focuses on the political difficulty that
humans have in agreeing on the importance of climate
change, and thus on the solutions. He sees no easy way
out of this conflict, which is battled out both between
nations (poor and rich ones) and within them.

Yet his suggested way out of the climate crisis brings
to light a new idea that he would surely have elaborated
further in future books: the suggestion that we cannot
wait for a complete solution before taking the first step
to change the world. Rather than despair at the idea
that, if the Chinese and the Americans do not change

their ways, changing our own behaviour is futile, we must start by changing what we can do, on our own level. This does not only, and perhaps does not even necessarily, mean changing the outside world. Above all, it means changing ourselves. 'It would be a mistake to counterpose thought and action', we read, for 'it's by doing things that we transform our imaginary. We have to start living differently, even if the initial gestures are symbolic, in order to learn how to invent a new world. We need to feel not just sadness about the old world that is crumbling, but joy for the possible future one.'

I have always admired Daniel for his ability to provide a comprehensive vision. He had a gift for painting a masterful tableau of the economy, politics and international relations with just a few brushstrokes. I believe that he always appreciated my determination to tackle 'small' problems as rigorously as possible, one after the other.

But, for a few years now, a doubt has been gnawing away at me: will this approach through many small steps suffice to deal with the vast problems that we are confronted with today? The last pages of this book clearly show that a mirror-image doubt was gnawing away at Daniel: that he could not describe any simple solution to the problems that he raised.

From the synthesis of these two concerns comes a new hope, his last gift to me (and to all of us). Daniel Cohen's ambition was immense, and so, too, are the objectives he sets for the reader in this book. The task is nothing less than to rethink work, our set of values, and international cooperation. But the only way that we can do this is to start this transformation of ourselves somewhere, at our own level.

Preface

What's left for me now is to try and fulfil, in honour of Daniel Cohen's memory, the project that he sets for us: 'It's up to us now to rethink our idea of a world in harmony with itself, one that makes us feel "a foretaste of happiness and peace".'

Introduction

Economic growth is the modern world's religion. It is the elixir that soothes conflicts. It is the promise of boundless progress. It offers a solution to the most basic drama of our human existence: wanting what we don't have.

So, we may well bemoan the fact that, today, growth has become an intermittent and elusive prospect. Bust follows boom and boom follows bust. Like the shamans who say they can make the rains come, politicians raise their hands to the sky to summon up economic growth – and then, when it doesn't arrive, they stir up people's resentment. But while the modern world is ever on the search for scapegoats, it skirts around the central problem: whatever would become of us if the promise of indefinite growth turned out to be an illusion? Would the world be able to find other satisfactions, or would it slump into despair and violence? We live in a time when, through the frenzied pursuit of material wealth, billions of human beings are jeopardizing the planet's very viability. In such a context, it is crucial that we think rather deeper.

Introduction

Writing in the 1930s, the great British economist John Maynard Keynes warned against the ambient pessimism of his day. His message of hope is still refreshing even now. Despite the looming crisis, Keynes warned against making the wrong diagnosis. Soon, he reassuringly insisted, the 'economic problem' would be solved, just as the problem of the food supply had been a century earlier. Extrapolating from what was then the current rate of industrial growth, he boldly predicted that, by 2030, people would be able to work three hours a day and devote themselves to the really important things: art, culture, metaphysics... Yet, we must sadly reckon with the fact that culture and metaphysical discussions have not become the main priorities of our time. Modern societies are, more than ever, devoted to the quest for material prosperity, even though they are by now six times richer than in the era when Keynes was writing. He was perfectly right to predict a future of prosperity. But even this great figure totally failed to predict what we would do with it. Like many before him, he was unable to grasp the extraordinary blindness of human desire, which is prepared to sacrifice everything to carve out a place for itself. 'Once primordial needs are satisfied, and sometimes even before that', wrote René Girard, 'man desires intensely, but he does not know what. For what he desires is being, a being that he feels deprived of and that someone else seems to have.' Growth is not a means to an end. It has become a goal in itself, allowing humans to escape the torment of our existence.

In his *The Accursed Share*, Georges Bataille analysed this curse that has reared its head time and again throughout the history of human societies: that is, their

Introduction

'need to go from all parts to the limit of the world's possibilities',[1] as if that were the only way to reach towards their truth. Can we shake off this curse? Can we face up to the challenge of climate change without having to endure chaos? These are the burning questions that we are forced to answer in a finite world. They take us on a long journey to understand human desire – and the different registers at which it has expressed itself throughout history.

---

[1] Georges Bataille, *The Accursed Share: An Essay on General Economy*, vol. 1, trans. Robert Hurley, New York: Zone Books, 1988, p. 133.

I

Genesis

The birth of the economy

Throughout much of humanity's existence, the only economic problem it faced was how to feed itself. From the dawn of time up until the invention of agriculture (which was only ten thousand years ago), humanity fed itself by freely drawing on whatever nature offered.

> We now know that peoples called 'primitive,' who know nothing of agriculture and stock breeding or who practice only a rudimentary agriculture, who sometimes lack a knowledge of pottery and weaving, and who live primarily on hunting, fishing, and the gathering of wild plants, do not have a gnawing fear of starving to death or anxiety about being unable to survive in a hostile environment. Their small numbers and their phenomenal knowledge of natural resources allow them to live in what we, no doubt, would hesitate to call abundance ... They have more leisure time, which allows them to make a large place for the imagination, to insert between themselves and the external world, as shock absorbers, beliefs, reveries, rites,

in a word, all the forms of activity we would call religious and artistic.[1]

This magnificent text by Claude Lévi-Strauss paints a vivid landscape of primitive societies, of the kind also hailed by the anthropologist Marshall Sahlins. As in the Garden of Eden, hunter-gatherer societies lived abundant and carefree lives, working just two to four hours a day to ensure the subsistence of all.

This ideal image of the societies of yesteryear must, nonetheless, be taken as a myth – one that we ought not be fooled by. What it does show, however, is human beings' incredible flexibility in their different ways of thinking about the world that they inhabit. This understanding of hunter-gatherer societies that knew nothing of toil and the accumulation of wealth is not as commonplace as Lévi-Strauss and Sahlins believed. There are many other models that differ from this. For instance, according to David Graeber and David Wengrow, 'Foragers in northwestern California . . . were notorious for their cupidity, organizing much of their lives around the accumulation of shell money and sacred treasures and adhering to a stringent work ethic in order to do so'.[2] People did not wait for agriculture before they began exploring all the possibilities of social life.

---

[1] Claude-Lévi Strauss, *Anthropology Confronts the Problems of the Modern World*, trans. Jane Marie Todd, Cambridge, MA: Belknap Press, 2013, p. 29.
[2] David Graeber and David Wengrow, *The Dawn of Everything*, London: Penguin, 2021, p. 148.

The agricultural revolution

Then, humanity learned to cultivate the land and to raise herds of animals. This is the moment when – to parody Rousseau's way of putting it – people decided to fence off a field and say: 'This is mine.' The invention of agriculture was a major shock that turned human life upside down. A period of global warming (around 9600 BC) may well have been the cause of this. Yes, even then. It began in the Fertile Crescent, the long strip of land stretching from the banks of the river Jordan to the Tigris and the Euphrates. Within a few centuries, barley and wheat were being cultivated there, with much larger seeds than the earlier wild versions. In less than a thousand years, agriculture became a science. People learnt how to use animals 'efficiently'. The idea was no longer to kill them immediately for their meat, but to breed them for their wool and milk, or to pull carts.

The invention of agriculture was not confined to the Middle East. At least three or four other sources can be identified too. The Neolithic revolution is thought to have taken place in China around 7500 BC, in Mesoamerica and the Andes around 3500 BC, and in eastern North America a thousand years later. Agriculture spread in several different ways. Sometimes, hunter-gatherers adopted it spontaneously, because it was more efficient. High technology drives out bad technology. Another way was more violent.

For example, Maori farmers used their greater numbers to exterminate their hunter-gatherer neighbours, the Morioris (in a region of what is now New Zealand): the force of numbers prevailed. The same pressure could be applied indirectly. Farmers destroyed the ecosystem that had allowed for hunter-gatherers' existence: wild animals fled, and wild plants became inaccessible. In all cases, whether by force or persuasion, a form of technological Darwinism was at work. The most powerful technology conquered everything in its path.

There are a few counterexamples, in those societies that endured. The Aborigines of Australia, though trading with neighbouring farmers, did manage for a long time to preserve their hunter-gatherer societies. But they are the exception to a rule that, for want of a better term, we'll call the *tyranny of productivity*.

The birth of civilizations

Abundance and a sedentary lifestyle allowed for food to be stored. The surplus made it possible to feed an 'idle class'. Kings, their bureaucracies, priests and warriors gradually detached themselves from the peasants. A process of innovation was now under way. Between 10000 and 7000 BC, humans became ever more the masters of stone materials, and farmers invented pottery, the first weaving machines, and architecture. Anatolian blacksmiths invented bronze in around 3500 BC, and iron tools by the end of the second millennium BC. Bureaucrats invented writing around 3000 BC in Sumer and around 1300 BC in China. Greek poets invented 'written vowels' around 800 BC. Between the thirteenth and ninth centuries BC, the hammering of bronze to make vases, helmets, breastplates and shields became a widespread technique; by this point, we are at the threshold of the world familiar to us from Homer's *Iliad*.

Discoveries were often made several times over in different locations (as in the case of writing or bronze).

Sometimes an identical copy was made by the societies in contact with the inventor. Such was the case of the alphabet. We could also say the same of the horse, which originally existed in only one place – Ukraine – and then travelled the world carrying warriors on its back, giving them a decisive military advantage. These discoveries raised human societies to new levels of social complexity. Chiefdoms became kingdoms and then empires. The great Sumerian, Egyptian, Minoan, Indian and Chinese civilizations were born in the wake of these inventions.

Malthus's law

Agriculture kick-started a demographic explosion that is still now ongoing. This has also crushed biodiversity, as other species have no way of adapting to our evolution in such a short period. Around 300,000 years ago, when modern man began his adventure, the total human population numbered in the hundreds of thousands – a million, at most. The first big turning point occurred between 40000 and 35000 BC. In that period, the population reached 4 or 5 million. With the advent of agriculture 10,000 years ago, the world population began a steep upward trend. With the emergence of the great civilizations of the Middle East, the human population rose to more than 10 million, and to 100 million by the time these civilizations collapsed around 1000 BC. The human population kept breaking new thresholds, reaching 250 million in the era of Jesus Christ, 1 billion in 1800, 2 billion in 1930, 8 billion today and, in all likelihood, 10 billion by 2050.

Whatever progress human civilizations have made, one implacable law applies: demographic pressure irresistibly cancels out the benefits of this progress. Progress in nutrition, and in hygiene and healthy living in general, has slashed infant mortality. Adults are also living longer, increasing women's life expectancy and the number of births. These two phenomena lead to an increase in the number of people in a given region. If each woman has six children who survive her – including, say, three daughters – then the population will double in size in less than a century. Overpopulation rapidly dilutes the benefits of abundant wealth. Demographic growth only stops when famine strikes. This is what we learn from Malthus's law: as humanity progresses, it is the *size* of the population that increases, rather than its *living standards*, on average at least.

As I have often emphasized, Malthus's law seems extravagant. Is it really possible that income has stagnated over the many millennia of human existence? This conclusion is, however, confirmed by the most recent work in quantitative economics. Gregory Clark makes bold comparisons on this score in his remarkable book, *A Farewell to Alms*.[3] He shows that the daily wage in Babylon (between 1880 and 1600 BC) represented fifteen pounds of wheat. In England, in 1780, it was almost at the same level, at thirteen pounds. Comparing British agriculture, one of the most productive in Europe in the eighteenth century, with 'primitive' societies, the results are even more striking. A British farmer in that era produced around 2,600 calories (of wheat, meat and fat) per hour. Many so-called primitive societies have done much better. The Kaulu in Indonesia produced

---

[3] Gregory Clark, *Farewell to Alms. A Brief Economic History of the World*, Princeton, NJ: Princeton University Press, 2007.

4,500 calories, the Mekranoti in Brazil 17,600. If we add to this, following Lévi-Strauss, that many hunter-gatherer societies only worked a few hours a week, we can see that the human condition deteriorated dramatically in the 10,000 years or so between the discovery of agriculture and the industrial era!

Dismal science

There is thus a key paradox in the history of agrarian civilization: agriculture, designed to feed people better, leads (everywhere) to a society where famine reigns. Seen in this light, the history of the economy appears to be a grim alternation of growth and crisis. Growth, when abundant resources have unleashed the forces of demography; crises, when the demographic momentum collided with the scarcity of resources.

Malthus's law has earned for economics the name of 'the dismal science'. For Enlightenment thinkers, such as Condorcet in France, poverty and misfortune were the result not of an 'evil' human nature, but of bad governments. While Malthus's father was an admirer of the Enlightenment, the son wanted to show exactly the opposite: that good government ultimately threatens public well-being. What *seems* good – peace, stability, public health – turns out to be a curse, because all these things encourage demographic growth and, ultimately, poverty. Conversely, the vices of war, violence and bad living create the opposite situation: they halt demographic growth, allowing a better life for those who do survive. For example, the great bubonic plague that swept across Europe from the mid-fourteenth century improved the economic situation of the survivors.

In the pre-industrial world, a high mortality rate was a good thing: it meant many fewer mouths to feed. To make matters worse, the Europeans of this era did not bathe. When the Globe Theatre was opened for the first performances of Shakespeare's plays, only one lavatory was provided for the 1,500 or so spectators! Patrons went to relieve themselves in the nearby park, or even in the theatre itself, on the stairs or in the corridors. The court of Versailles was also notorious for its appalling smell.

Whatever the mores of the day, ultimately the planet is populated by a growing mass of starving humans. The more solutions we find, the worse the problem gets. The world's population doubled every thousand years over the last eight millennia, then began to double every century, then every half-century. The term 'demographic bomb' has been used to describe this deadly acceleration, in which the ever-greater number of techniques devised to overcome malnutrition in turn exacerbate the problem that must be solved on an ever-increasing scale. In the 1960s, an extrapolation was made based on the trends of the twentieth century. The study concluded that the Earth's population was set to explode – and, by 13 November 2026, would become infinite.

Demographic transition

But the demographic explosion did not take place. Humans ended up – as a last resort, we might say – reducing the number of children born per woman. This is known as the 'demographic transition'. The 10,000-year parenthesis in which population growth governed human lives is coming to a close. After ten millennia during which agricultural societies built up a regime of subordinating women to the demographic imperative, birth rates finally collapsed.

This process began in Europe at the end of the eighteenth century and then spread throughout the world. In the space of just a few decades, from 1870 to 1910, fertility declined in almost all European countries, at the same time and almost independently of socioeconomic variables. For example, Britain and Hungary began their demographic transition at the same time, even though they had very different levels of education and infant mortality. Illiterate and rural Bulgaria also began its transition in this same moment. The fact that this all took place in the same era leaves little doubt that this had to do with a far-reaching cultural shift, rather than a simple reaction to socioeconomic changes, for instance the ones bound up with urbanization.

The same dramatic turning point can be seen in developing countries after World War II. Fertility fell in just a few decades, from an average of 5 children per woman in 1950 to 2.4 today. The same rule applied to all societies and across different religions. In Brazil – a devoutly Catholic country with a long history of high population growth – the fertility rate fell in less than twenty years from 4 children per woman to 2.3. Between 1950 and 2000, Egypt saw its fertility rate fall from 7 children to 3.4, and Indonesia from 5.6 children to 2.6. In India, over the same period, fertility rates fell from 6 children per woman to 3.3. The explanation given by United Nations demographers echoes analyses of the demographic transition in Europe. The sources of change are cultural. Women watching television all over the world have found a fascinating model: that of Western women whose way of life (as seen on TV, at least) has become an aspiration to freedom. Brazilian *telenovelas* have proved to be stronger than the Church, which had hitherto put up powerful obstacles to family planning. The demographic transition is properly explained in terms of a change in mentality, not a change in financial incentives. If we want to conceive what place we might have in a desirable future, we need to imagine a change of a similar nature: another shift from quantity to quality.

2

Prometheus Unbound

The Industrial Revolution changes everything

So, around the middle of the eighteenth century, Europe took a turn so important that its magnitude can properly be compared only to an event like the Neolithic Revolution. The Industrial Revolution shook up the structure of human life to a degree that would have been unimaginable even a few decades previously. It interrupted humanity's immemorial sojourn in the land of Malthus.

As its name suggests, the Industrial Revolution was driven by the emergence of new industrial techniques. The most famous of these was James Watt's steam engine, which completed a series of innovations initially aimed at improving mine pumping. Still, with the advent of the steam engine, the world learned to do a lot of things more than just pump water from mines: there soon came the railways, then steamships... The mechanization of the world was about to begin in earnest.

Aristotle famously summed up slavery by explaining that if 'the shuttle would weave and the plectrum touch the lyre without a hand to guide them, chief workmen would not want servants, nor masters slaves'.[1] The history of the British textile industry offers an especially good window on what the future had to say about his prediction. In 1733, a genius textile-maker by the name of John Kay invented the flying shuttle – the same kind as the one Aristotle had dreamed of 'weaving without a hand to guide it'. Kay perfected an automatic shuttle return system, which made it possible to weave widths greater than the span of the weaver's arm. Thanks to his invention, the speed of work doubled. The result? Kay was immediately chased out of his home city of Colchester. Chased from town to town by rioters who realiszed that the shuttle was going to take 'their' jobs, he died in poverty, banished to France.

However, Kay's discovery gave the British textile industry an advantage that would endure for almost a century, alone explaining almost 50 per cent of British growth in the first half of the nineteenth century. The sequence of events is spectacular – and a perfect example of how capitalism works. Outside Colchester, Kay's machine spread, dramatically reducing costs. The heightened rate of weaving meant that spinning also had to keep pace. But the old spinning wheels were too slow. Yarn delivery times increased, as did prices. It wasn't until 1764 that another brilliant inventor, Richard Arkwright, perfected a spinning machine – the water frame – which allowed his workers to operate eight and then sixteen and then sixty spindles at a time,

---

[1] Aristotle, *Politics*, 1254a, trans. Benjamin Jowett.

using hydraulic power. To step up the motor force of his looms, in 1777 he called on the services of James Watt, whose steam engine was then honed for this purpose.

As the textile industry developed, it encountered new bottlenecks, in the bleaching of hung cloth. In the past, fabrics had been bleached with curdled milk and dried in the sun. For that, you needed lots of meadows and lots of cows. The entire chemical industry set to work to solve this problem, and soon produced radical innovations. The first step was to switch from cow milk to soda ash. But soda ash was produced from a rare plant, glasswort, which was in short supply during the wars fought by post-revolutionary France and the Napoleonic Empire. The process developed by the Frenchman Nicolas Leblanc was gradually adopted. Chlorine, which had first been isolated in 1774, became the basis of bleaching.

But white is one thing, and colour quite another. The race to develop the dye industry became the big business of the nineteenth century. The first synthetic dye, marketed in 1856, was the work of an English chemist by the name of W. H. Perkin. It allowed Queen Victoria to wear a superb mauve at the 1862 International Exhibition drawing the envy of chemists across Europe. German industry was born of this challenge. In 1869, it synthesized alizarin, which replaced the madder plant, grown in Vaucluse, as the basis for red colours. Thanks to the exceptional profits it generated, the industry stepped up its research, with the quest for scientific understanding bound up with the thirst for profit. Finally, it reached the holy grail: synthetic indigo, which came to market in 1901. It also invented aspirin, in

1899, leading to the development of the modern pharmaceutical industry.

By this point, we are a far cry from John Kay's early troubles. But the sector that he created offers a good insight into the logic behind industrial innovation. The principle is always the same: the growth race pushes the sectors that are lagging behind to breaking point, triggering innovations that break the previous balance and sometimes set off along an independent course. One imbalance comes hot on the heels of another, but ultimately this race drives overall growth.

Britain was a unique case, where growth rested on a few cutting-edge sectors: textiles and steel to start with, then mechanical engineering and shipbuilding, while relying on exports to find market outlets. Britain also went much further than other countries in terms of the regional polarization of different activities: cotton in Manchester, mechanical engineering in Glasgow, and so on. Britain provided the mould for what would much later become the Asian model. On the European continent, and in France in particular, progress was slower. Mechanization developed gradually, and craft production persisted for longer. A century later, however, the result was the same: industrial society had replaced rural society.

Coal and slaves

The Britain of the eighteenth and nineteenth centuries would experience a tremendous demographic boom, perfectly in line with Malthus's prediction. The British population rose from 7 million in 1701 to 8.5 million in 1801 and 15 million in 1841. So, how did Britain manage to feed this new population – and avoid the Malthusian trap? This is all the more mysterious given that the new technologies were slow to find useful application in the agricultural sector. It was not until the final third of the nineteenth century that advances in the chemicals industry led to the development of fertilizers, or that the internal combustion engine allowed the replacement of horses by tractors. How did Britain withstand the demographic shock? The answer is simple. It consisted of importing agricultural produce in exchange for industrial products. Britain adopted the model that would later be adopted by the newly industrialized countries in the 1970s and by today's China: a wholly export-driven growth strategy, in a first phase focused on the textile industry in particular, the revenues from which would pay to import agricultural produce that would otherwise be lacking.

By 1830, exports of industrial goods accounted for half of all British production. The domestic market could never have provided enough outlets for the production that took place in Britain, and the land available in Britain could never have sufficed to feed the workers or provide the natural fibres that industry needed. Britain relied on Canada for timber, and Australia became its main supplier of wool. New products were also imported – such as jute from India and palm oil from West Africa.

The other great reservoir of natural resources on which Britain drew was the United States. The bid to exploit the virgin lands of the New World came up against a problem, however: the fact that they were abundant also meant that they were sparsely populated. Manpower was scarce there, and thus expensive. Who would farm these new lands? There was a grimly famous solution: and one that Africa had to provide. A triangular trade was set up. Britain sold textiles to Africa, which exported slaves to America, which exported cotton to Britain. Robert Fogel and Stanley Engerman demonstrated the effectiveness of this system in a book that was to revolutionize the historiography on the subject: *Time on the Cross*.[2] According to some estimates, slaves produced two-thirds of all American exports to Britain, with sugar and cotton the main goods concerned. While the dearth of slaves marked the decline of the Roman Empire, it was the abundance of African slavery that enabled the British Empire to flourish.

In addition to imported natural resources, Britain also benefited from an inestimable domestic resource located deep underground: coal. It offered an unhoped-for alternative to traditional energy sources, all of which depended directly or indirectly on available land, whether that meant agricultural land to feed people and animals, or forest land for wood-based energy. Britain, which was running out of forests, was lucky enough to have an abundance of coal, which became the main energy source for the burgeoning textile industry. But it was also the fuel for the new means of communication – the railway and, above all, the steamship – which conveniently linked the two sides of the Atlantic, bringing Britain closer to its markets and suppliers. The circle was complete. The 'Promethean' miracle would have come to nothing had it not been for Britain's coal reserves, American land and African

---

[2] Robert Fogel and Stanley Engerman, *Time on the Cross. The Economics of American Negro Slavery*, Boston, MA: Little, Brown and Company, 1974.

slaves. Malthus's law was overcome, in hardly glorious fashion.

The great thinkers

Towards the middle of the eighteenth century, economists began to consider the possibility of an economy that would be governed entirely by markets. The key author, who set the terms in which economics is still thought about today, was Adam Smith. His theories were set out in his famous book *An Inquiry into the Nature and Causes of the Wealth of Nations*, published in 1776.

Smith presents labour as the key to the wealth of nations (rather than gold or land, as had previously been thought). In a well-known example, he explains that, in a society of hunters, the price of a beaver can be compared with that of a deer by calculating the ratio of the time needed to kill each of them. If it takes twice as long to kill a deer, its price will necessarily be twice that of the beaver. If it were worth less, hunters would immediately stop pursuing deer. The same reasoning would apply to beavers in the opposite case.

In a more elaborate version, however, the market does more than this. The division of labour that it encourages makes it possible to increase workers' productivity. In the famous example of the pin factory (taken from a visit to Normandy that he made when he was private tutor to a young aristocrat), Smith noted that ten workers managed to produce 48,000 pins a day, whereas one worker, left on his own, could make no more than 200. By centralizing pin production, the productivity of each worker was multiplied twenty- or thirty-fold.

What limits this process, Smith explained, is the size of the market. The division of labour is a brilliant idea, but you still have to find someone to sell the 48,000 pins to. If demand is only for 200 pins a day, it would be better to employ just one worker, even if this means lower productivity. However, it is quite conceivable that, as wealth increases, an endogenous process of productivity rises will be set in motion. The richer the society, the greater the division of labour, the higher the productivity, and the stronger the growth. *Indefinite* enrichment becomes a possibility.

The example of the pin factory led Adam Smith to wish for the sphere of the market to be as large as possible. He thus called for the liquidation of non-market activities (domestic activities) and expressed the hope that as many of them as possible would be swallowed up by the market. As the advertising slogans say: everybody wins, both buyers and sellers.

This pioneering thinker wanted to show that, thanks to the market, everyone can specialize in some job or other – doctor or lawyer, butcher or shoemaker – without having to worry about running out of goods that they do not produce themselves. This unspoken cooperation, this 'invisible hand' that binds together the participants in the exchange, is based on a simple factor: everyone has an interest in it. It was this idea that inspired Adam Smith's famous phrase: 'It is not from the benevolence of the butcher, the brewer, or the baker, that we expect our dinner, but from their regard to their own interest.'

Smith was here as much a philosopher as an economist. At the time when he used the word 'interest', it did not yet have the neutral meaning that it has since acquired to characterize economic calculation. As Albert O. Hirschman, himself an economist and philosopher, brilliantly shows in his book *The Passions and the Interests*, it was long synonymous with greed, featuring prominently in Dante's *Inferno* alongside pride and envy. Smith, in a work published before *The Wealth of Nations* and titled *The Theory of Moral Sentiments*, showed that he himself had no illusions about the scope of the term:

> What is the purpose of all the toil and bustle of this world? What is the purpose of avarice and ambition, of the pursuit of wealth, power, and pre-eminence? . . . Well, then, what is the source of that emulation – that trying-to-copy – that runs through all the different ranks of men? What advantages do we expect from that great purpose of human life which we call bettering our condition?

Smith's answer is what Hegel would call the desire for the other's desire: 'The only advantages we can aim to derive from it are being noticed, attended to, regarded with sympathy, acceptance, and approval. It is the vanity – not the ease or the pleasure – that draws us.'

The author who inspired Smith was a certain Bernard Mandeville, who in 1705 published *The Fable of the Bees*, with the telling subtitle: 'Or, Private Vices, Publick Benefits.' The conclusion he reaches is a whole worldview: 'So Vice is beneficial found, When it's by Justice lopt, and bound; Nay, where the People would be great, As necessary to the State As Hunger is to make 'em eat.' By showing that ambition, vanity and the need for attention can be satisfied by improving material conditions, Smith could set out his theory of the 'invisible hand', according to which: 'Without any intervention of law, therefore, the private interests and passions of men naturally lead them to divide and distribute the stock of every society among all the different employments carried on in it; as nearly as possible in the proportion which is most agreeable to the interest of the whole society.'

Karl Marx tackles 'capital'

Marx is the author who analyses capitalism from the other standpoint: that of the victims. 'That boy of mine', says a woman whose story he relates, 'when he was 7 years old I used to carry him on my back to and fro through the snow, and he used to have 16 hours a day . . . I have often knelt down to feed him as he stood by the machine, for he could not leave it or stop.'[3] Marx – who published his masterpiece, *Das Kapital*, a century after Smith – could see capitalism driving a vast transformation of British society right before his eyes. The market was not the promised factor of universal enrichment, but the tombstone over the working classes. Far from creating a society at peace, it provided the weapons for a civil war – the class struggle.

Marx brought the working-class condition into economics textbooks. Industrial labour had become a miserable reality. To grasp how capital exploits labour, Marx introduced a crucial separation between labour as such and 'labour power'. Suppose it takes a beaver hunter ten hours to kill this animal: the price of the beast will be, as Smith says, the monetary equivalent of ten hours' work. The snag is that there is no guarantee

[3] Karl Marx, *Capital*, vol. I, London: Penguin, 1976, pp. 356–7.

that the hunter himself will be paid this sum. If he is hired by a capitalist, how much will the latter have to pay him? The hunter's wage must be at least equal to the cost needed to feed, clothe and house him – in short, to enable him to work – and this is the price of his 'labour power'. Does the capitalist have to pay more? No, as long as there are enough workers ready to take on the job to avoid dying of hunger.

In this case, it would be enough to pay the minimum rate. Let's say it takes the equivalent of four hours' work to feed a worker, and the worker can work ten hours: the difference is the 'surplus value' that the boss can pocket. This surplus value, this surplus labour, is the source of profit.

Marx was convinced that capitalism could only generate profits if it kept the proletariat destitute: 'In proportion as capital accumulates, the situation of the worker, be his payment high or low, must grow worse.'[4] Indeed, '[the bourgeoisie] is unfit to rule because it is incompetent to assure an existence to its slave within his slavery.'[5] Malthus made demographic pressure the main reason for this sinister equilibrium. Marx imported Malthus's theory into the industrial world, through a new idea: the industrial reserve army of labour. In order to impose low wages, as a source of surplus value, capitalism needed to maintain a mass of unemployed proletarians, forcing those who had jobs to accept subsistence pay rates. In place of demographic pressure, capitalism substitutes a poverty which it itself creates for

[4] Karl Marx, *Capital*, vol. I, London: Penguin, 1976, p. 799.
[5] Karl Marx and Friedrich Engels, *The Manifesto of the Communist Party*, in *Marx and Engels Collected Works*, London: Lawrence and Wishart, vol. 6, 1987, p. 495.

the sake of its own proper functioning. Although Marx repeatedly paid tribute to the bourgeoisie for having abolished millennia of aristocratic power in the space of a few decades, he concluded that the bourgeoisie itself is headed for extinction, once its inability to develop what he calls the 'productive forces' seals its historical failure.

Joseph Schumpeter

So, how was it possible for capitalism, despite everything, to make workers richer? To answer this question, economists reworked their intellectual tools. To the two factors of production, labour and capital, analysed by Smith and Marx, they added a third factor of production: 'technological progress'. This theory owes its rise to approaches inspired by the Austrian-born economist and Harvard professor Joseph Schumpeter and, many years later, by the MIT economist Robert Solow.[6] As Solow explained, technological progress enabled the same worker to do in one hour what would have taken ten hours a century earlier. It's as if, behind the work apparently being done by just one person, several 'humanoids' are silently working away on their behalf. When I send an email, I'm sending a message on my own that would once have taken several days of human labour. Technical progress makes workers more productive, which ultimately allows for them to be paid more.

As Schumpeter also predicted, technological progress is a double-edged sword. It is both a creative and

---

[6] Joseph Schumpeter, *Capitalism, Socialism and Democracy*, London: Routledge, 2003 [1942]. Robert Solow, *Growth Theory: An Exposition*, Oxford: Oxford University Press, 2000.

destructive force, and it's easy to cross the line from the one to the other. This is Schumpeter's most famous phrase: capitalism brings about a 'process of industrial mutation ... that incessantly revolutionizes the economic structure from within, incessantly destroying the old one'.[7] It is both an accomplice to the workers and their executioner, helping those who survive its purge to earn more. It is, give or take, Darwin's idea of natural selection, now applied to industry.

[7] Joseph Schumpeter, *Capitalism, Socialism and Democracy*, London: Routledge, 2003 [1942], p. 83.

3
Prosperity and Depression

The 1929 crisis was global capitalism's darkest hour. The crisis spread from Wall Street to Europe and then to the rest of the planet. Even today, leaders around the world remain haunted by the events of 1929.

This crisis cut short a decade of brilliant growth in the United States, the so-called Roaring Twenties. In France, these were the *Années folles,* or 'wild years'. The elements of modern consumer society, and of the American way of life, were spreading far and wide, from the automobile to electricity, cinema, radio, and more. Car production tripled, from 1.9 million vehicles in 1919 to 5.9 million in 1929.

On 4 December 1928, Calvin Coolidge delivered his last message to Congress as President of the United States. He concluded his address with a triumphant tirade: 'No Congress of the United States ever assembled, on surveying the state of the Union, has met with a more pleasing prospect than that which appears at the present time.' The stock market wavered both up (like in 1924) and down (like in 1926). But it was from the beginning of 1927 that speculation ran riot. In the spring of that year, the governors of the banks of England, France and Germany came to the United States to ask its monetary authorities to make a move to relieve the European economy. They got their wish. The US's own central banking system – the Federal Reserve Board, colloquially known as the Fed – lowered its discount rate from 4 per cent to 3.5 per cent. According to Lionel Robbins, a professor at the London School of Economics at the time, it was from 'that date, according to all the evidence, the situation got completely out of control'.[1] Between 1926 and 1929, stock prices doubled. The euphoria spread to small savers. According to a joke told by John Kenneth Galbraith, which reflects the spirit of the times, 'the rich man's chauffeur drove with his ears laid back to catch the news of an impending move in Bethlehem Steel'.[2] In other words, he was eavesdropping for sensitive information about Wall Street.

Gradually, however, from 1928 onwards, the Fed raised its rates to break what Alan Greenspan – who would one day be its chairman – would much more accurately call the 'irrational exuberance' of the financial markets. In January 1929, the rediscount rate had already returned to 5 per cent. On 14 February, the New York Fed proposed raising the rate from 5 to 6 per cent to stop speculation. A lengthy controversy ensued. Rates were not raised until the late summer of 1929, when they were finally upped to 6 per cent. But the

---

[1] Lionel Robbins, *The Great Depression,* New York: Transaction, 2009, p. 53.
[2] J.K. Galbraith, *The Great Crash, 1929,* Boston, MA: Houghton Mifflin, 2007, p. 77.

increase came too late, at the worst possible moment. By the early autumn, the US economy was already in crisis.

The crash

Thursday 24 October is the first of the famous days that history identifies with the panic of 1929. On that day, known as 'Black Thursday', 13 million shares were traded, well above the usual daily average of 4 million. By 11.30 a.m., the market was gripped by panic. Eleven traders had already committed suicide. Outside, a mysterious hubbub could be heard and crowds gathered. At midday, New York's leading bankers – Charles E. Mitchell, president of National City Bank, Albert H. Wiggin, president of Chase National Bank, William C. Potter, president of the Guaranty Trust Company, and Thomas W. Lamont, senior partner at JP Morgan – all met. These grand masters of finance set about turning the market trend around by buying up the shares. Once the news got out, prices immediately rose. The *Times* hailed the news, noting that 'the financial community' was now 'secure in the knowledge that the most powerful banks in the country stood ready to prevent a recurrence [of the panic].'[3]

Yet the following Tuesday – 29 October, known as 'Black Tuesday' – the panic resumed, this time unstoppably: 16 million shares were traded; stock prices plummeted. It was the start of the spiral that was to lead to the abyss. The following Thursday, 31 October, the Fed lowered the rediscount rate from 6 per cent to 5 per

---

[3] Cited in J.K. Galbraith, *The Great Crash, 1929*, Boston, MA: Houghton Mifflin, 2007, p. 105.

cent. But it was to no avail. The fall continued. The first low was reached on 13 November 1929. Stock prices had already lost half their value. Over the next three years, Wall Street lost 85 per cent of its September 1929 market capitalization.

The United States now experienced a recession of unprecedented scale. Industrial production halved between 1929 and 1932. Unemployment hit a quarter of the active population.

The first source of growth to fall away were purchases of durable goods (cars, furniture, washing machines, and so on.). These goods are intrinsically sensitive to economic cycles. You have to eat every day, but you can put off buying a car or a washing machine. When everyone does the same thing at the same time, the sector collapses. But a further aggravating factor also came into play. The preceding years had seen the introduction of consumer credit, revolutionizing American consumer habits: 85 per cent of furniture, 80 per cent of phonographs and 75 per cent of washing machines were financed on credit. At the time, goods bought on credit were seized in the event of default, regardless of payments already made, which made consumers even more cautious when faced with a crisis. By 1930, the consumption of durable goods had fallen by 20 per cent, and it slumped by 50 per cent between 1929 and 1933. Car purchases plummeted by two-thirds between 1929 and 1932.

A crisis in real estate was the other factor that overturned the macroeconomic equilibrium. The construction boom had in previous years done much to fuel growth. This sector had more than doubled by 1926, compared with pre-World War I levels. The turnaround was all the more spectacular. As in the case of the durable goods market, the credit cycle was an aggravating factor.

Farmers were collateral victims of the crisis. Unlike other sectors, their situation had not been brilliant up to that point. Since the end of World War I, overproduction had been the rule. During the war, the area of cultivated land in the United States had expanded to compensate for the drop in production in the belligerent countries in Europe. As peace returned, excess supply had a lasting effect on prices. Farmers' net incomes collapsed, falling by 70 per cent between 1929 and 1933. This tragedy was immortalized in Steinbeck's novel *The Grapes of Wrath*.

And the financial crisis appears ...

Another crucial factor has also been highlighted in order to explain the sheer scale of the crisis: bank failures. In the monumental *Monetary History of the United States* that he wrote together with Anna Schwartz, Milton Friedman showed how the crisis precipitated the collapse of the banking system, which in turn worsened the crisis.[4] The fall in economic activity jeopardized banks' balance sheets, which made depositors nervous. Losing confidence in the most vulnerable banks, depositors withdrew their deposits, effectively pushing them into bankruptcy. In three years, from 1930 to 1933, half of all American banks disappeared. There were 29,000 banks in 1929. By the end of March 1933,

---

[4] Milton Friedman and Anna Schwartz, *A Monetary History of the United States*, Princeton, NJ: Princeton University Press, 1963.

only 12,000 remained. Between 1929 and 1933, the US money supply contracted by one-third. The banking crises deprived businesses, especially small ones, of their sources of finance, and in turn forced them into bankruptcy. Farmers, small and medium businesses and indebted households were directly affected. In his own research, Ben Bernanke, who became the Fed's chairman in 2007, showed that the bank failures make it possible to anticipate, almost month by month, the United States' plunge into recession.

And yet the tragedy was that the monetary authorities barely reacted to this situation. Noting that interest rates were very low (between 1 and 2 per cent), they did not feel obliged to inject additional liquidity to save the banks. According to Friedman's interpretation, this was the main cause of the disaster. The monetary authorities of the time were not up to the task. They stood idly by as the banking system collapsed, believing that it was not part of their mandate to save a bank that had failed. It was not until February 1932 that President Hoover, who had famously predicted in 1930 that recovery was 'just around the corner', created a Reconstruction Finance Corporation, with public capital, to offer advances to financial institutions in difficulty.

An international crisis

The crisis of 1929 would never have reached the dimensions it did if it had not contaminated the entire planet. International trade shrank dramatically. Global imports fell from 3 billion in April 1929 to 1 billion in February 1933. The US authorities' errors regarding banks in their own country were coupled with equally tragic errors in the area of trade policy. In 1930, the US Congress voted in the Hawley–Smoot tariff. This provided for a 40 per cent increase in duties on wheat, cotton, meat and industrial products. The crisis in the United States then spread to international trade, with the countries affected by the American measures rushing to take retaliatory measures.

The economic crisis also created a raw materials crisis that endangered exporter countries. Prices collapsed between 1929 and 1933, to a third of their initial level. To free themselves from the burden of their debt, most Latin American countries defaulted. Only Argentina resisted the temptation to do so – surprising as that may seem from today's perspective – at the cost of a much more severe depression than was suffered elsewhere.

But the key factor was the crisis in the international monetary system. The US financial earthquake quickly spread to Europe, mainly as a result of the imbalances inherited from World War I. Plans to reschedule the German war debt followed one after another (in 1924 with the Dawes Plan, and in 1929 with the Young Plan) with no solution found that was up to the scale of the challenge. It was not until the Lausanne Conference in 1932 that the Allies realized the futility of 'making Germany pay'. Shortly after the resignation of Chancellor Brüning, Germany finally extracted the financial concessions that ought to have been granted much earlier.

Rather like the depositors pulling their money out of the US banking system, international capital fled from countries that it considered vulnerable. There was a wild dance among the different currencies. In May 1931, when the major Austrian bank Credit Anstalt went bankrupt, it caused a wave that than crashed over banks in Hungary, Czechoslovakia, Romania, Poland and Germany. Then it was the United Kingdom's turn to be at the heart of the turmoil. The Bank of England's gold reserves suddenly seemed insufficient, and on 21 September 1931 it abandoned the gold standard. The dollar was also under threat, prompting US authorities to adopt a cautious stance – also partly explaining the unresponsiveness criticized by Friedman. Then it was the French franc's turn. When the Popular Front came to power, capital that had found a haven in France fled the country.

Throughout this period, monetary authorities sought to reassure depositors and speculators by keeping their currencies convertible into gold for as long as possible. This also forced them to adopt a series of restrictive policies in order to reduce their financing needs. Conversely, as soon as a country abandoned the gold standard, growth resumed and capital flooded in! This was the case in the United Kingdom from 1931, in the United States from 1933 and in France a little later. The paradox of this era was that the still-burning trauma of postwar inflation made monetary authorities extremely anxious about abandoning monetary orthodoxy and reviving inflation, even as their economies were subject to severe deflation.

Keynes, the iconoclast

No contemporary government understood the true nature of what had happened in 1929. Most remained convinced that the first thing to do was to restore confidence by maintaining balanced public finances and the gold convertibility of their currencies. In following this course, they all made the depression worse. Like Molière's doctors who recommend bloodletting, their cures weakened and sometimes even killed the patient. It was not until the publication of Keynes's book, *The General Theory of Employment, Interest and Money*,[5] that economists finally had a framework for thinking about this new subject: macroeconomic equilibrium.

In truth, Keynes was a heterodox author. He had already made a name for himself with the publication in 1919 of *The Economic Consequences of the Peace*, in which he denounced the Treaty of Versailles and the draconian conditions imposed on Germany. He called for a 'general bonfire' as a way of clearing away the debts built up during the war, so that it would be possible to start afresh on a sound footing.

Say's Law

In his *General Theory*, Keynes went to war against what is known as 'Say's Law', named after the early-nineteenth-century French economist. Say summed up his doctrine in a famous phrase: 'Supply always creates its own demand.' We sell one commodity because we intend to buy another. If I sell my labour, or my chickens, it's to meet a need and create a demand that matches my sales. Supply and demand interact. There can be no permanent imbalance between the two.

But in the real world, things don't work like that. If there is a reduction in demands for a car, the company

[5] John Maynard Keynes, *The General Theory of Employment, Interest and Money*, London: Palgrave Macmillan, 1936.

that manufactures cars will lay off its employees, who will no longer express the same demand that they previously might have done. An imbalance is created: consumption is reduced, and so are jobs. Impoverished by the redundancies, households will consume even less. This gloomy climate will not encourage companies to hire. The initial imbalance will be *multiplied*, perhaps considerably. Unemployment will take hold because, in all sectors, supply will outstrip demand.

The Keynesian remedy for underemployment was thus a simple one: spend, and spend at all costs, even if it meant hiring the unemployed to fill in the holes they had dug that same morning. This was the lesson that Keynes drew from the Great Depression. Capitalism left to its own devices is profoundly unstable, yet it can be regulated through a shrewd economic policy. When postwar politicians set about stabilizing the economy, Keynes's remedies served as their catechism. The fact that the proposed solution was to consume rather than save was no small factor in the success of these ideas. They laid the foundations on which the welfare state would be built.

The welfare state

In November 1940, at the height of the war, Churchill commissioned a report to combat the social consequences both of the crisis of the 1930s and of the conflict itself. The report was published in 1942. William Beveridge set out the principles we share today. The state had a responsibility to combat the five scourges of humanity: 'idleness, ignorance, disease, squalor and want'. Convinced by Keynes that not spending enough

could only make society poorer, Beveridge felt justi-
fied in demanding that social spending should be as
universal as possible. Hence the title of his report: *Full
Employment in a Free Society*.

The welfare state was not, strictly speaking, his invention. The idea predated the 1930s and – even without
here delving into the details of its initial development
– we can give credit to Otto von Bismarck for being one
of its main founders. In 1883, the German Chancellor
passed one of the first pieces of social legislation aimed
at workers, introducing compulsory health insurance
for low-paid workers. Bismarck famously said: 'Sirs,
the democrats will play the flute when the people realize
that the sovereign is looking after their interests better.'
By the eve of World War I, the United Kingdom, France
and the United States had all passed social legislation of
some kind.

The twentieth century saw a massive expansion of
the role of the state. Each of the two world wars played
a crucial role in this regard. Rising military spending
forced governments to raise taxation to unprecedented
levels, and it would not come down again afterwards.
After, first, World War I and, again, World War II, social
spending slowly but surely replaced military spending.
Society increasingly demanded the rights to education, healthcare and pensions. Although Keynesianism
helped to explain why this development was indeed
economically desirable, the rise in social spending was
mainly driven by need – for healthcare, and for old-age
insurance – rather than by an orthodox regulatory plan.

4

The Golden Age, and its Crisis

Legendary years

In 1946, in a village called Douelle, in Quercy, France, you had to work twenty-four minutes to buy one kilo of bread, forty-five minutes for one kilo of sugar, seven hours for one kilo of butter, and eight hours for one kilo of chicken. Food accounted for three-quarters of total consumption, half of it made up of bread and potatoes. On average, meat from the butcher was bought and eaten only once a week. Butter was virtually unknown. More than half of the rest of personal consumer spending went on clothing. Apart from heading off on military service, the vast majority of inhabitants had only travelled for their honeymoon and for a few pilgrimages.

Thirty years later, in the same village, the productivity of agricultural labour was twelve times higher. A kilo of butter now took only one hour and twenty-five minutes to produce. In 1946, Douelle had a population of 534, with 208 farmers, 12 non-agricultural workers, 27 artisans and 32 service sector employees. In 1975, out of 670 inhabitants in the same village, there were only 53 farmers, 35 non-farm workers, 25 artisans and 102 service workers. In 1946, two babies under the age of one died every year; by 1975, only one died every two years. In 1946, the average twenty-year-old man was 1.65 metres tall; by 1975, the average was 1.72 metres. In 1946, three new houses were built every twenty years; by 1975 the rate had increased to fifty. One year after the end of World War II there had been five cars in Douelle; by 1975, there were almost 300. We could cite many such indicators of how life changed over these three decades: two televisions became 200; no washing machines became almost 200, and five refrigerators became 210.

This famous example is described at the start of Jean Fourastié's now-classic work *Les Trente Glorieuses*.[1] Far beyond this one village, the whole face of France changed over the thirty years between the end of World War II and the mid-1970s. Like Douelle, France went through all the stages of modern economic growth, in other words the transition from agriculture to industry and from industry to services, in an extremely compressed space of time.

Douelle is emblematic of the transformation of a society where most resources had once been devoted to ensuring the food supply, but in which people now watched TV and headed off on holidays. Through this example, Fourastié unveils what can be considered his major discovery (Colin Clark offers a similar example for the English-speaking world). The modern world is

---

[1] Jean Fourastié, *Les Trente Glorieuses*, Paris: Fayard, 1979; new edn in Hachette's 'Pluriel' series, 2004.

not simply a transition from a rural to an industrial society. It is in fact tending towards a third stage: a service-based society. In his famous first book, *Le Grand Espoir du XXe siècle*,[2] he identified what he saw as the true meaning of progress: 'Everything proceeds as if human labour were in transition from physical effort to cerebral effort.'

The oil crisis

Throughout the postwar decades, the rate of growth averaged around 5 per cent each year. This means that French people's incomes doubled every fifteen years. A young man starting his career in 1945 with an income of, say, €2,000 in today's money would have earned €4,000 in 1960 and €8,000 in 1975, when this three-decade period came to an end. This tells us something about how traumatic it would be when this growth regime came to an end.

The break came with the oil crisis. The OPEC countries quadrupled the price of oil in 1973 and doubled it again in 1978. This spectacular rise in oil prices set economies on the path to a new and initially little-identified evil: 'stagflation', an unprecedented mixture of inflation and recession. Economists and politicians were slow to understand this phenomenon properly. Trained since the end of the war in Keynesian ways of thinking, they had learned to analyse economic cycles as the expression of imbalances stemming from final demand. When demand is low, there is unemployment

---

[2] Jean Fourastié, *Le Grand Espoir du XXe siècle*, Paris: Gallimard, 1963 [1948].

but inflation tends to fall. When demand is too high, the opposite happens: unemployment falls and inflation rises. This inverse relationship would be described in terms of the so-called 'Phillips curve', named after the economist who highlighted this phenomenon in 1956.

Stagflation turned these ideas on their head. For now, *both* unemployment *and* inflation were on the rise. It took some time to understand this seeming paradox. The spike in unemployment was not caused by insufficient demand. The problem was that supply had suddenly stopped being profitable, first because of the rise in the price of oil, but also because of a more permanent factor, namely the slowdown in technical progress. All the governments that tried to combat unemployment by boosting consumption – in France including the ones led by Valéry Giscard d'Estaing and François Mitterrand – failed. All they managed to do was to accelerate inflation.

The rise of the hardcore economic liberals

The oil crisis paved the way for a powerful challenge to Keynes's thinking. Politicians and economists replaced him with a new *maître à penser*: Milton Friedman, the leading thinker of the Chicago School. These economists advocated that the state should rein in its role. Friedman denounced the welfare state as the culprit behind firms' loss of competitiveness. He insisted that the market was infallible, and unemployment a 'natural' phenomenon. In his view, Keynesian economic policies worsened the very problem that they were meant to combat. By trying to achieve full employment at all costs, they prompted an acceleration in inflation, which could then be curbed only at great cost.

The defining event in this sequence was the monetary policy pursued in the early 1980s by Paul Volcker, chairman of the US Federal Reserve. In a bid to rein in inflation, he abruptly reduced the money supply, triggering an explosion in interest rates. Under the effect of his shock-therapy measures, US inflation fell sharply between 1982 and 1984. At the cost of a considerable recession, the 'credibility' of US monetary policy was finally restored, and confidence in the dollar returned. Faith in Keynesian precepts had disappeared completely! This was the climate in which the so-called neoliberal revolution of the 1980s unfolded.

5
The New Financial Capitalism

The new age of inequality

However, the neoliberal doxa also faced a serious obstacle: the fact that, after the crash of 1929, the stock market had carried both a moral and an economic stigma. It had been widely held responsible for the crisis and for World War II. Company directors acted on the basis of what they thought was best for their businesses, while brazenly overlooking considerations of shareholder interest. This was the era of what we might call managerial capitalism. The Cold War also played its part in this regard. As the philosopher Peter Sloterdijk humorously puts it, this was a period when workers could easily get their demands met: 'It sufficed for them to consider the realities of the Second World [the Soviet bloc] to make it clear to the employers that social peace has its price.'[1]

Starting in the 1980s, shareholders reasserted control

[1] Peter Sloterdijk, *Rage and Time*, New York: Columbia University Press, 2012

over how businesses were run. The kind of organization of work that had predominated in the postwar period – with its career plans, its social-policy measures and its trade unions – was increasingly called into question. Bonuses replaced career plans. If in this period managers had been employees rather like any other, they now rapidly broke out of this condition. Their fate and their incomes were now increasingly indexed to the stock market – and they obeyed its logic, for they were themselves part of it. This period saw the death of one type of capitalism and the birth of another.

This new 'shareholder capitalism' dictated a different norm, which reduced companies' activities to their own particular know-how: their 'core business'. Everything else would have to rely on the market. Outsourcing became the rule. In a company in the 1950s and 1960s, the canteen, security, cleaning and accounts would all be handled by in-house staff. With the financial revolution of the 1980s, none of these services was delivered in-house: instead, service providers competed on the market. Some even dreamed of companies without employees! This process was accelerated by the revolution in information and communication technologies. This trend was completed by the advent of globalization, which broadened the space of competition and allowed a cheaper labour supply. The outsourcing of tasks gave way to offshoring, wherever possible. But let's be clear about the chronology: the internal reorganization of capitalism preceded globalization.

The invention of Fordism had transformed the contemporary imaginary. Trade unionism had won its victories at the heart of a strongly organized industrial world created by Fordism. In the new regime that took hold in the 1980s, everything was done to break any unity among workers. The piece-by-piece sell-off of the large industrial complexes of the past was aimed in particular at breaking trade-union counterpower.[2] Design offices sectioned off engineers and graduate workers in their own world. Maintenance departments did something similar for their unskilled counterparts. Everything was done to ensure that each social class lived among themselves alone, with no more 'organic' links between the different levels of society.

The work of Thomas Piketty and his co-authors has shown the incredible explosion of inequalities in this new world of production.[3] Over the course of fifty years, the bottom half of the population has seen its share of national income shrink from 20 per cent to 10 per cent. During the same period, the richest 1 per cent went in exactly the opposite direction: their share rose from 10 per cent to 20 per cent.

This rise in inequality contrasts dramatically with the postwar years, when growth in purchasing power was almost identical at all levels of society. But while income disparities between the extremes have returned to nineteenth-century levels – cancelling out in just a few decades their twentieth century reduction – inequalities within individual firms have changed relatively little. It is the inequalities between companies and between design offices and cleaning departments that have really exploded. In the past, engineers and maintenance staff belonged to the same firm. Salary increases for the former were automatically passed on to the latter

2 Philippe Askenazy, *La Croissance moderne*, Paris: Economica, 2002.
3 Thomas Piketty, *Capital in the Twenty-First Century*, Cambridge, MA: Harvard University Press, 2013.

because they were bound by the same pay scales. The new situation, with personnel atomized into their different spaces, no longer fostered this equalization of wealth. The 'trickle-down' of wealth announced by Reagan and Thatcher was systematically blocked from the early 1980s onward, by this orchestrated social distancing. What were the consequences of this?

The subprime crisis

The conservative revolution would have an unexpected effect, as it fundamentally changed the financial system. A new form of financial intermediation developed, completely unbound from the rules laid down after the 1929 crisis. This new reality is sometimes called the 'shadow banking system'. Starting from almost nothing in the 1980s, by the eve of the financial crisis it counted for as much as the traditional banking system in the United States, i.e. some $10 trillion. This system includes hedge funds, private equity funds (which buy unlisted companies on credit) and insurance companies. The banks themselves have created new structures, known as 'special investment vehicles' (SIVs), located off-balance sheet to avoid prudential rules.

In its own way, market finance is fulfilling Wall Street's new dream: to create firms 'without factories and without workers'. Traditional banks have the onerous task of collecting retail deposits through their branches. They have to prepare customer files for all loan applications, following them over time until they reach maturity, and bear the risk of default. What modern finance did was to free itself from these nuisances! Firmly attached to their computer screens, its players – the traders – would finance themselves solely on the market, ignoring the constraint of having to collect deposits from individuals. Instead of granting loans, they 'securitized' them, i.e. put the loans granted by others on the market, after having first reorganized them. This new system outsourced all the traditional functions performed by commercial banks, such as collecting deposits and distributing loans, and prospered on its own sole core business: financial engineering. The stage was thus set for the biggest collapse in financial history.

The subprime crisis was triggered by several time bombs. First of all, it soon became apparent that the quality of loans had deteriorated dramatically, even taking into account the new customer base at which they were aimed. The creditworthiness of customers was systematically overestimated by the intermediaries responsible for handing out loans. The cause of this deterioration is obvious. With the securitization of loans, the originator of the credit immediately sells it on to the financial markets. The incentive structure is totally changed. What counts is making a profit, not monitoring the quality of the borrower. In addition to such negligence, there is also proven evidence of fraud. Some lenders artificially inflated the creditworthiness of their customers in order to improve their balance sheets.

With the help of rating agencies, investors then produced instruments that were deemed risk-free, with AAA ratings. To this end, they used sophisticated mathematical models that predicted the probability of default for a given type of debt, so as to extract the least risky part. Yet such models led the mighty Goldman Sachs to close down a fund whose probability of default had been estimated at one in ten to the power of one hundred and thirty-eight! In fact, market finance led to the circulation of 'false financial money', securities whose quality has not been verified as it should.

The spectre of 1929

When the subprime crisis erupted in summer 2007, the Fed chairman was undoubtedly the person best qualified to deal with it. Ben Bernanke was the author of academic papers that helped to decisively establish the responsibility of the US monetary authorities in the crisis of the 1930s. His research won him the Nobel Prize in 2022. Right from the start of the crisis in summer 2007, he was ready to inject huge amounts of liquidity into the economy, and showed no hesitation in rescuing the investment bank Bear Stearns and then the major mortgage refinancing agencies Freddie Mac and Fannie Mae.

Yet even Bernanke ended up making the mistake that he denounced in his books. By allowing Lehman Brothers to go bankrupt on Monday 15 September 2008, he triggered the shockwave that set off the explosion. Like Black Tuesday in 1929, it was the bankruptcy of Lehman Brothers that really fired the starting gun on the crisis. All corporate paymasters realized that the refinancing of their loans, which had been more or less ensured over the previous year, would no longer be guaranteed. Firms began to sell off inventories and to cut back on investment. Households' confidence was shattered.

However, the spectre of 1929 did then play a crucial role. Everything was done to save the endangered banks. Considerable sums were quickly mobilized under the

Paulson plan ($700 billion) to avoid further disasters – along the way stirring up the popular feeling that the bankers' past vice was being rewarded. The subprime crisis was a certain reminder of the power of Keynesian reasoning. Without the authorities' determined intervention (notwithstanding their fault for the Lehman Brothers collapse), the situation would probably have degenerated. Less than a quarter of a century after the financial revolution, which thought it possible to 'forget '29', crisis had returned looking much the same.

The mirage of a world left to the whim of market forces alone has, in fact, been abandoned.

6
Globalization

The East India Company, the first multinational

In the mid-1970s, huge blocs of the world's population in India, China and Latin America were still largely closed off from international trade. Then, quite suddenly, between the death of Mao Zedong and the fall of the Berlin Wall, most of these regions opened up to trade and found, through it, the path to economic growth. To understand this great turnaround, we need to go back to the foundations of theories of trade, such as they were conceived and put to work in the nineteenth century.

The great theorist of international trade, David Ricardo, explained that the exchange between nations is like the exchange between people as analysed by Adam Smith: it drives forward the division of labour. A normally established individual will practise one single trade. You can be a baker or a shoemaker, but rarely both at the same time, even if you might have been perfectly suited to both careers. I might be an excellent baker as well as a marvellous shoemaker, but I'll choose the trade that will earn me the most: making bread, or making shoes. Applied to the scale of nations, this principle explains, according to Ricardo, why a country has to choose the sector in which it will excel; this is not an absolute choice, but some relative priority has to be given to one of the available options.

At the dawn of the nineteenth century, this choice seemed clear. Britain had to specialize in industry, particularly textiles, where it was well ahead of other nations. Other countries, logically enough, had to make the exact opposite choice – namely to 'de-industrialize' and specialize in agricultural or mining sectors, where they had a comparative advantage over Britain. That's exactly what happened. However, the Indian textile industry represented between 65 and 75 per cent of total British manufacturing activity. At the beginning of the nineteenth century, Indian textiles, particularly calico, which was highly prized in London, accounted for up to 70 per cent of India's total exports. But as the century went on, all would be lost.

India, an emerging power

Trade between India and England was conducted under the aegis of a British firm: the East India Company, a unique example of a private company controlling a country. Contrary to Ricardo's theory, the East India Company initially prohibited India from exporting its textiles to Britain, fearing that India would get the upper hand. It was only at a later period, with the consolidation of Britain's industrial advantage, that free trade was imposed on the Indians. English textiles flooded into India, completely destroying the local craft industry. India then lost its foothold in the industrial field and specialized in products in which it did indeed have a 'comparative advantage': jute, indigo and opium. Indeed, this latter narcotic was exported to China, which was itself expected to provide tea. When China, worried about the effect on its population, tried to ban opium imports, Britain launched the so-called Opium War to force China to open its ports.

It was based on this traumatic experience that poor countries developed their immense resentment of free trade and Ricardo's theories. Upon achieving independence, the overwhelming majority of 'developing' countries would, as a matter of course, embark on the path of economic protectionism. In fact, as they all pointed out, this was the path that France, Germany and the United States had spontaneously chosen to take when faced with the rise of British industry.

The Japanese model

However, there is a counterexample to the deindustrialization of poor countries: Japan. It was the only country that had begun the twentieth century poor but then joined the club of rich countries. It was this model that was later emulated by the so-called Four Asian Tigers: South Korea, Taiwan, Singapore and Hong Kong. In light of their success, in the 1980s emerging countries revised their ideas on international trade. Perhaps it was finally time for them to use such commerce to their own advantage: to industrialize, to the detriment of the rich countries themselves. These emerging countries' choice would be made easier by the fact that their rich counterparts were also calling into question their own production model. With the financial revolution, they demolished the previous model in favour of a new organization of industry that was heavily reliant on subcontracting, whether at the local or the international levels.

The famous Barbie doll is a remarkable example of what has been called the 'vertical disintegration' of the manufacturing process. The raw materials, plastic and hair, come from Taiwan and Japan; assembly is done in the Philippines before moving to lower-wage areas such as Indonesia and China. The moulds come from the United States, as does the final touch of paint before sale. Barbie pushes the quest for the lowest cost to its extreme consequences by leaning as much as possible on subcontracting.

The new international division of labour

In Ricardo's language, what took shape here was a new division of labour between rich and poor countries: the latter would be responsible for the manufacture of industrial products, while the former would be responsible for what came both upstream (their conception) and downstream (marketing and sale). We find a marvellous illustration of this in Nike sneakers: designed in the United States, manufactured in Indonesia and marketed all over the world.

Let's look more closely at the price of a pair of Air Pegasus trainers. They retail at $70. First question: how much does the worker – most likely a woman – who makes them earn? The answer: $2.75. Whatever we learn about the rest of the cost structure, one conclusion is clear enough already: the producer's work has become a very small part of the value of the final product. It's a far cry from Adam Smith's theories.

Let's continue to break down the cost structure. There are more surprises in store. To make a shoe, you need not only labour, but also raw materials: leather, rubber, etc. You also need to buy machinery, rent warehouses and repay the capital that has been invested. Then the product has to be exported. In plain terms, the pair of sneakers costs Nike $16.50 to make. Nike then transforms the physical product into an object of desire. It launches phenomenal advertising campaigns. The cost of promotion per pair (including paying star talent and the advertising campaigns themselves) is $4. To this must be added the work of Nike's own employees (administration, reps, etc.) as well as the company's capital expenditure, payment for investments, storage costs and shareholder remuneration. It's worth pointing out that Nike is not an especially profitable company. In total, the wholesale price of a pair – the price at which Nike sells them to distributors – is some $35.50. The remainder, which doubles the price, comes from the cost of distribution, putting the shoes on the feet of the end buyer. You have to pay the staff who sell them, rent the shops, and so on.

An object like Nike's Air Pegasus thus costs as much to manufacture as a *social* object as it does as a *physical* object: Nike spends as much on promotion as it does on production in Indonesia. What's more, it costs as much to put the shoe on the consumer's feet as it did to make it available and desirable. This example is a fascinating illustration of the 'new world economy'. It is made up of 'immaterial' production (the brand), designed for the city and the world; of material production, i.e. the shoe, which comes from afar; and, representing the dominant share, services in the narrow sense, i.e. putting the product thus produced at the consumer's feet, in her home, in her streets.

China returns

The history of China is a good illustration of this transformation of modern capitalism. It offers an impressive example of a country that was for a long time the most powerful in the world, then one of the poorest, and now once again one of the richest.

Let's go back in time to the year AD 1000. Back then, China was ahead of the West in virtually every field. It had already mastered the iron plough and the crossbow. It was familiar with lacquer, the kite (including man-lifting kites), the compass, paper, steel, the use of oil and natural gas as fuels, and also harnesses for horses, the wheelbarrow, canals for inland navigation, and more. A fascination with magnetism led the Chinese to discover the compass, which allowed them to embark on bold ventures at sea. Almost a century before Christopher Columbus, Admiral Zheng He set off to discover Africa at the head of a formidable fleet of seventy ships and thirty thousand men. The vessels are said to have been 138 metres long, 55 metres wide and with nine masts.

In fact, in the fourteenth century China experienced an industrial revolution quite similar to the one that Britain would launch some four centuries later. Thanks to an agricultural revolution, linked to the use of much higher-yield rice from Vietnam, China began a period of rapid urbanization. There was development in textile and steel making. The Chinese had long understood the principle of atmospheric pressure. From a strictly technological point of view, they ought to have been perfectly capable of developing the steam engine. So, why didn't they?

According to US economist Kenneth Pomeranz, the main cause of the divergent destinies of China and Britain was due to an accident of geography. The north and north-west of China had (and still have) vast coal reserves. The Chinese had mastered the process of transforming coal into coke (purified coal). The country produced more coal for the purposes of metal-working in the year 1000 than Europe (excluding Russia) did in 1700. But the Mongol invasion at the beginning of the fourteenth century turned it upside down. By the time China regained a degree of stability after 1420, the country's demographic and economic centre had shifted to the south. Coal-mining resumed in the north, but never again became a dynamic sector on the frontier of innovation. The potential users of coal in the south and the producers in the north were like ships passing in the night.

Added to this explanation is another, cultural one.[1] After the turmoil that followed the Mongol invasion, the search for domestic stability became a priority and the concern to explore the wider world took a back seat. Despite the zebras and giraffes brought back from Africa by Admiral Zheng He, the emperor decided that these voyages were too expensive. What conclusion did he draw from this? He had the fleet burned down! China was increasingly trapped in a perspective of philosophical and political immobility, which reached its peak under the Qing dynasty.

---

[1] David Landes, 'Why Europe and the West? Why Not China?', *Journal of Economic Perspectives*, 20(2), 2006.

This policy – unsurprisingly – discouraged trade and industry, but encouraged corruption and nepotism. The state controlled everything, from trade to education, in what we would today call 'totalitarian' fashion. An atmosphere of routine, traditionalism and immobility made all and any innovation suspect. While in Europe the rivalry between the different powers was itself a stimulus to innovation, China did not have such an impulse. Preoccupied with its own internal stability, it broke off its dynamic of progress, even though it had earlier been far ahead of Europe. China opted for stability and retreated into itself.

Europe took a quite different route.

The great metamorphosis

Five centuries later, the speed at which China has moved, since Mao's death, from an economy cut off from the rest of the globe to one of the economies most open to trade, is stunning. It is by now the world's third largest exporter, behind the United States and Japan, but ahead of Germany. The country's trade surpluses have enabled it to accumulate vast foreign exchange reserves, putting it far ahead of other industrial countries and on a par with the major oil exporters. China's cash reserves are equivalent to the entire French GDP. These reserves give China the means to become a new power. It is financing Africa and organizing a new Silk Road to secure its supplies.

Extrapolating current growth rates, China will probably become the richest country in the world at some point between 2030 and 2050. This expected return to the top is most obviously due to the size of its population. In terms of per capita income, China remains a poor country. In international rankings, it is on a par with Egypt, or the standard of living of an American in the year 1913. If in, say, 2050, China were to become the richest country in the world, it would by then have the same per capita income as the United States in the 2000s. So, measured in terms of years, China would have been a century and a half behind the US in 1990, but just half a century behind in 2050.

China's strategy, strongly inspired by the Japanese example, can be summed up in three major areas. The first is to stimulate exports. Boosting exports is the policy approach consistently followed in most Asian countries. Adam Smith explained that the most important ingredient in sustainable growth lay in the development of markets, the lack of which was the main handicap for the poor countries. The world market is a way around the problem of having domestic markets that are too small. This was the strategy adopted by Britain in the nineteenth century.

A second aspect of China's Japanese-inspired policy is intensive education. The Maoist strategy of massive school enrolment is bearing fruit here. Launched in the mid-1950s, it enabled China to reduce the illiteracy rate to one-third of the population by the early 1980s. This policy was subsequently strengthened by a law passed in 1986, which set a minimum of nine years' compulsory education after the age of six. Even today, there may well be more Chinese who speak English than there are native speakers!

The third factor is a very high savings rate, at close to 50 per cent of income. This makes it possible to finance investment at a frenetic pace and to build up considerable foreign reserves. This plethora of savings frees the country from the constraint that has long hampered growth in emerging countries, particularly in Latin America, namely a shortage of capital of its own.

The new reserve army

China is experiencing both a spectacular fall in the number of very poor people (defined as those living on less than $1 a day) and an equally spectacular rise – in inequality. China has, in its own way, taken up Marx's theories on the industrial reserve army, as it relies on the mass of workers ready to leave the countryside and move to the cities.

Following the classic patterns of rural exodus that have dominated in the past, particularly in Europe, peasants leave the countryside for the cities and settle there permanently. The first generations suffer, as Marx's accounts describe, but their children eventually integrate into urban life. The Chinese system is designed in such a way that migrants are virtually obliged to 'return home' to start a family. It is based on the so-called *hukou* system, which assigns each person a registered place of residence, which is the same as their mother's. This iron rule determines rights of access to public goods: children, for example, can only attend state schools or have access to healthcare in their parents' official *hukou*. It is thus almost impossible for a 'migrant worker', i.e. one living outside their allocated area, to start a family. In the city, they are on her own, exploited at will – and here, I mean 'exploited' in the sense Marx used the term.

'Upon somebody's inquiring timidly what was the cause of her anxiety, she had answered solemnly: "I'm worried about China".'[2] Madame de Guermantes's famous line in Marcel Proust's *In Search of Lost Time* is back on the agenda. In 2020, in the early days of the COVID crisis, China was presented as a model of pandemic management, rigorously pursuing the 'test, trace, isolate' trilogy. By 2022, it had become the laughing stock of the world. By stubbornly pursuing a zero-COVID policy based on rigid quarantines, it turned its back on a policy of intensive vaccination which, in those countries able to afford it, offered a much better solution.

The COVID-19 crisis took China back thirty years, to the fork in the road represented by the bloody repression at Tiananmen Square in 1989. By crushing the demand for democracy, the authorities had, perhaps strangely enough, paved the way for a rapid acceleration of capitalism. Yu Hua, the wonderful author of the novel *Brothers*, captured the significance of this perfectly in his book *China in Ten Words*. He explained how, once the path of democracy had been stifled, the regime had encouraged unbridled enrichment to compensate for political frustrations. Yu Hua noted ironically that Westerners tend to think that capitalism and democracy go hand in hand. In the case of China, it was one instead of the other. Enrichment has become an alternative to the demand for personal freedom and civil liberties

The post-Tiananmen era, followed by China's entry into the World Trade Organisation (WTO), brought the country a period of brilliant GDP growth, averaging around 10 per cent a year. Even before the COVID pandemic, however, there was a marked slowdown,

[2] Marcel Proust, *The Fugitive*, New York: Modern Library, 1993, p. 779.

with growth halving in the space of just a few years. There are many reasons for this. First, the country is exposed to the risk that all emerging countries face when they cross a certain threshold of wealth, the so-called middle-income trap. As they become richer, they lose the comparative advantage of low labour costs that enabled them to build up their position on international markets. China's ageing population, a consequence of the one-child policy, is also holding back the dynamism of the labour market. Many experts also think that the growing footprint of state-owned enterprises poses the risk of Sovietization.

Whatever remedies may be found, it is clear that China has entered a new, slower phase, similar to what France experienced at the end of the Trente Glorieuses once the euphoria of postwar reconstruction had passed. As rapid growth recedes, the political management of the system will run into the same difficulties as those encountered by the industrial countries, without having recourse to trying, democratically, to explore other options.

China is still a cause for concern.

7

The Digital Revolution

Homo numericus

In one of the most memorable episodes of the hit British TV series *Black Mirror*, a young woman loses her husband, killed in a car accident on the day that she learns she is pregnant with his child. Thanks to the artificial intelligence (AI) that scans her late husband's phone conversations, videos and emails, he is digitally resurrected in perfect detail. He is back with the same intonation and intuitions, as well as the answers to the questions she has been asking herself. *Black Mirror* is such compelling viewing because the worlds it portrays seem like they might be just around the corner. It explores our ability to accept the power of new technologies, rather than their limitations, assuming that the relevant obstacles are now less technical than they are social and psychological.

The idea that we can resurrect the dead by tapping into their 'history' is utterly terrifying and entirely credible. Software powered by AI delves into the personalities of its users. By recognizing the intonations of their voices, the complexion of their faces, and identifying the patterns and limits of their vocabulary, they capture the moods and aspirations of each individual. Many job and university recruitments are now carried out online, with AI pre-selecting the few candidates from a list of applicants that might number in the tens of thousands; those who pass this filter will have the chance to meet a human examiner in the home straight. Love is no exception. Apps like Tinder make it possible to industrialize romantic relationships by reducing the time spent wooing partners.

Completely unexpectedly, the COVID-19 pandemic served as a catalyst for this great transformation. The winners of the crisis were Amazon, Apple and Netflix, companies whose market capitalization exploded during the crisis. They have made it possible to work remotely, to buy goods without having to go to a shop, to be entertained without having to go to a theatre or a concert hall. Remote medicine has also taken off, given that the relationship between the sick person and the caregiver does not necessarily require the patient to be actually present in the doctor's surgery. A new way of conceiving the world of production has emerged, a far cry from previous practices. The need to meet face-to-face with colleagues or clients has become one option among others. The aim of digital capitalism is plain for all see: to reduce the cost of physical interaction as much as possible, to dispense with the need to meet face-to-face. To generate returns, it is necessary to dematerialize human relationships, stripping them of their flesh and blood.

The Digital Revolution

The great hope of the twenty-first century?

Online, everything is being done to slash the costs of entertainment, education, healthcare and dating. In order to understand the nature of this transformation, and the coincidence of its acceleration with COVID-19, we need to look back to another text by Jean Fourastié. He authored this work in 1948, long before he wrote *Les Trente Glorieuses*, but it provides a crucial key to understanding that period. In this text, Fourastié heralded the transition from an industrial society to a service society as 'the great hope of the twentieth century'.[1] After the agrarian societies that cultivated the land and then the industrial society that moulded materials, he explained that, in the service society, humanity would finally cultivate itself. Education, health and leisure would be at the heart of the new world.

Fourastié announced: 'The tertiary civilization will be brilliant; half or three-quarters of the population will benefit from higher education. Initiative at work, even at the bottom of the hierarchy, and the diversity of means of transport and leisure activities, will, in the course of a few generations, encourage man's individualistic tendencies.' Thus, he concluded:

> The time is coming when history will have advanced far enough that human beings can legitimately strive to elaborate the philosophy of the new age, and work in a less oppressive darkness toward a dramatic birth. In liberating humanity from the labour that inanimate matter can

[1] Jean Fourastié, *Le Grand Espoir du XXe siècle*, Paris: Gallimard, 1963 [1948].

execute on its behalf, the machine must lead us toward jobs that man alone among all Creation can perform: those of intellectual culture and moral improvement.

Upon the book's publication Léon Blum, left-wing former prime minister, wrote an enthusiastic review. For Fourastié, this transition to a 'humanized' society also heralded a world without economic growth. For if the commodity that I am selling is the time I spend with others, then, unless I am always working more to earn more, growth must come to an end. A doctor who treats a patient, a teacher overseeing a class, an actor who fills a theatre: all these jobs that are characteristic of the service society are hampered by the absence of productivity gains that would enable us to do in one hour what we used to do in two.

The industrialization of services

The digital revolution is thus the lever that will enable the service society to become more productive. In economic terms, it can be said to be 'industrializing the postindustrial society'. This is, on the face of it, a contradictory expression used to describe the rationalization process aimed at reducing to a minimum the cost of human interaction, which is at the heart of the third age that Fourastié is so keen to see coming to fruition.

There are several methods. Television is an example of a technology that multiplies the number of customers of a single service-provider, in this case the actor. This is known as achieving economies of scale. Another method is the one we see in the case of remote medicine. There is still a provider and a customer who meet face to face, but not necessarily in the same place. Only the essential meetings are kept going. The key question is, of course, that of deciding what really is 'essential'.

To save money, you can also replace the service provider with an algorithm and leave the customers to fend for themselves. This is the case when you need to manage your online bookings or bank accounts without an assistant. Software can already take care of all the tasks normally entrusted to an assistant: from making appointments to booking plane tickets or collating computerized accounting records. So-called intellectual professions actually spend a lot of time doing things other than their core business. According to one estimate, 60 per cent of a researcher's time, for example, is diverted from research work by administrative tasks. The next stage in the development of artificial intelligence is one in which the algorithm will be able to take the initiative: book your hotel when it detects that you have an appointment in another city, take minutes of meetings in which you took part, communicate with other machines to prepare a conference . . .

Another example is call centres. For the most part, they have been relocated to poorer countries, whether that means from the US to other English-speaking countries or from France to French-speaking ones. The precise codification of these tasks – entrusted to people who have no knowledge of the questions they are being asked – is made possible by the so-called Pareto principle, which tells us that the range of questions asked is in fact very limited. For example, if the most frequent question represents 50 per cent of the total, the second will be 25 per cent, the third 12.5 per cent and so on. In this case, three questions cover more than 85 per cent of cases. It is this work of codification that first allowed the response to be outsourced to foreign service providers, and today allows computers to take the place of humans.

That's why we spend countless hours pressing 1 or 2 or 3 to get an answer from an answering machine (my television's broken, what should I do?) before we reach the holy grail: a human being, who will only appear as a very last resort. Even then, the person who answers will often repeat the same digitized protocol before directing you, if necessary, to a real technician.

This process is also now reworking medicine. Medical algorithms are able to extract the relevant elements for analysing a given symptom from an almost infinite library of data and articles. Dermatologists already know how to make the most of the millions of images that have been analysed and diagnosed, enabling them to find appropriate references immediately. Above all, it serves as an aid to their diagnosis – for the moment. Radiologists are under greater threat. Their job is to take X-rays and offer an interpretation of them to their colleagues. AI will be able to provide this initial diagnosis itself, leaving it to the doctor who ordered it to listen to the opinion of the few specialists who have survived the digital purge, if she deems this necessary.

The industrialization of services also imitates the rationalization process seen in factories, except that here it is the consumer who is directly 'Taylorized'. Unmanned shopping centres have already been created, notably for Sunday opening. You walk in, help yourself and walk out. Facial recognition mechanisms will identify you, debiting the credit card that you have registered beforehand (we can imagine that you will have the possibility, if you really want, to check the expenses that have been billed to you). The idea of entering a totally dehumanized shopping centre makes the blood run cold, but the next stage is already in place, with Amazon, which will dispense with the need to physically move around.

The age of the thinking robot

Fittingly enough, the fantasy of anthropomorphic robots has an ever stronger grip on the contemporary imaginary. An analogy can be made with the development of vision 500 million years ago. Sight helped to prompt the multiplication of living species on Earth. Robots are perhaps in the process of reaching this stage. Error rates in labelling photo content fell from more than 30 per cent in 2010 to less than 5 per cent in 2016, and are now below the human error threshold. Progress in voice recognition has been just as spectacular. Apple's Siri, Google's Assistant and Amazon's Alexa use new interfaces to recognize spoken words, interpret their meaning and respond accordingly. Vaughan Pratt also points out that digital machines have the revolutionary ability to instantly share their knowledge with each other.

Building on these advances, researchers are working on the creation of so-called soft-touch robots, which interact with humans in a feel-good way. Japan is at the cutting edge of all these fields, given its rapidly ageing population. The booming home automation sector is preparing for this, digitizing homes with sensors to monitor elderly or dependent Japanese people's state of health and any falls they might suffer. The presence of robots in their apartments should also enable carers to remotely control their patients for tasks such as administering medicines or taking temperatures, or quite simply to offer medical staff a full field of vision, as long as the robot can accompany the patient into the corners of their lives. Emotional dialogue is the main remaining challenge for AI designers. Recognizing and simulating emotions, using voice, face and gesture cues, constitute the current focus of the development of what are also called chatbots.

Recruiting and judging

AI is increasingly widely used in hiring and recruitment processes. Universities are already using algorithms to assess applications, taking into account the schools that prospective students have attended, perhaps giving special credit to those who can list their extracurricular activities. In the private sector there is already an established practice of conducting an algorithmic interview with the candidate, judging both content and form: ease of diction, smile, empathy. So-called applicant tracking systems have forged partnerships with most job-related websites, such as LinkedIn and Monster.com. You will soon be automatically contacted by recruiters, without having to do anything other than create a full-colour, video CV on which you can be judged.

In the film *Elysium*, a dystopia brought to the screen by Matt Damon and Jodie Foster, algorithms go even further: policing and the justice system are entrusted to robots that follow a rigorous protocol. The robot-judge calculates the probability of reoffending and sets a sentence accordingly. The robot offers Matt Damon the chance to appeal to another human, but he rejects the offer for fear of a harsher punishment. This is only sci-fi, but the book *Noise*, written by Daniel Kahneman and his co-authors, presents a concise and coherent argument that can be interpreted as a plea for algorithmic justice. The starting point of their analysis is an implacable demonstration of the fallibility of human judges; they are just as affected by their moods as any other human beings. An analysis of several thousand court rulings showed that judges take harsher decisions on the Monday following the defeat of the local (American) football team! In France, an exhaustive study likewise showed that judges are more lenient on the defendant's birthday (Kahneman mischievously adds that the hypothesis that judges are also more lenient on their own birthdays is still to be tested). Juries are also prey to statistical fallacies. For example, they find it harder to grant asylum to a migrant if they have already granted it to two previous applicants.

Judges are also highly sensitive to the outdoor temperature. Several studies of hundreds of thousands of cases have shown that convictions are harsher on hot days. Academic boards and hiring committees are no exception to this influence from the weather. When the weather is average, university decision-makers pay close attention to the academic quality of the applications: grades, quality of dissertations. But when it's nice out, they are more concerned with the candidates' nonacademic qualities. Doctors are just as vulnerable to this kind of effect. At the end of a long day at work, they are much more likely to prescribe opiates than they would at the start of the day, as if their own fatigue applied to the patients they are examining.

Faced with these errors of judgement, algorithms offer an alternative that is not subject either to the time spent on the task or to the outdoor temperature. One team of researchers trained AI to simulate conditional releases of offenders. This team had access to the same information as judges, particularly concerning the defendant's criminal record. To avoid stereotypical judgements, no data on gender or race was provided to the computer. Relative to judges, AI significantly improved the quality of judgements. Bail decisions made by AI are said to have reduced the crime rate by almost 25 per cent, assuming a constant incarceration rate. Researchers at MIT have also shown that it is possible to reduce the incarceration rate by 40 per cent for a given recidivism target. As soon as the objective is simple to state in statistical terms – in this case, to reduce the average rate of recidivism – AI clearly wins out over human decision-makers.

The Taylorization of affect

Beyond AI, the digital revolution is just one in a long line of radical innovations that have changed the way that human beings think.

For instance, the invention of writing marked an irrevocable break between 'savage thought',[2] as Lévi-Strauss called it, and societies where history is established through the written word. At the dawn of modernity, the invention of printing also brought about a true intellectual revolution, promoting freedom of thought and contributing to the rise of the Reformation. We would love it if AI took its place in this glorious

2 [TN: In French, *pensée sauvage*, a pun on 'wild pansy'.]

lineage, helping us to think better both individually and collectively. Unfortunately, the opposite seems to be happening. The transformation under way is giving rise to a credulous and uncritical individual. We were expecting Gutenberg, but what we got was Benjamin Castaldi.[3] In other words, television 2.0 is taking over.

Michel Desmurget, in *La Fabrique du crétin digital*,[4] has done a marvellous job of analysing the disruption caused by the digital revolution. The numbers that he provides are enough to make your head spin. At the age of two, children spend almost three hours a day in front of their screens. Between the ages of eight and twelve, they spend an average of four and three-quarter hours a day in front of tablets and mobile phones. Between the ages of thirteen and eighteen, this rises to six and three-quarter hours a day. In other words, teenagers spend 40 per cent of their waking hours in front of a screen! The psychological and emotional lives of these young people are patterned by waves of gloom and euphoria, with harmful effects on their diet and often the risk of obesity. Scrolling, impulsiveness and impatience strongly affect teenagers' attention spans. Reading a book – which requires granting the author at least the time to establish the characters or a way of seeing things – is constantly interrupted by the compulsive return to the mobile screen, which makes it impossible to concentrate on anything else.

Marshall McLuhan, the high priest of the subject, said that the 'Medium is the message': the media are

---

[3] [TN: a French TV presenter and host of light entertainment shows.]
[4] Michel Desmurget, *La Fabrique du crétin digital. Les dangers des écrans pour nos enfants*, Paris: Le Seuil, 2019.

their own content, and it's television that we watch, not any particular film. In the same way, we don't know what we're watching on our mobile phones: indefinite scrolling is utterly addictive. It's scrolling itself that draws us in, whether it's images of a child watching *The Lion King* or news about the war in Ukraine or the Middle East. The iPhone creates a real fusion of man and machine. The tactile interface creates a relational, addictive link between the two, like hard drugs that take hold of the brain and subjugate it to the need to consume them. A phone ringing summons exactly the same part of the brain as when someone's first name is spoken. Even when the mobile is switched off but within sight, the need to switch it on, to feel it in your hands, is as irrepressible as the fix in the brain of a heroin addict.

Our compulsion to look at our phones has been labelled with a now well-known term: FOMO, the Fear of Missing Out. It expresses the nagging anxiety about missing out on something, whether it's news, gossip or some opportunity. Teenagers' real-world attention span has hit an all-time low. According to a study quoted by Bruno Patino, it fell by one-third between 2008 and 2015, from twelve seconds to just eight. An experimental study tested the impact of a smartphone on an audience that previously did not have one. In less than three months, it recorded a clear deterioration in attention spans, with a notable worsening of responses to arithmetic tests. 'Impulsiveness' has also increased, in nigh-on direct proportion to the amount of time spent on the smartphone. A comparable study conducted by a team at Stanford deactivated access to Facebook for a month. The time freed up enabled them to see more of their family and friends, and watch more television.

Ultimately, there was a significant improvement in the well-being of the test subjects – and once the experiment was over, their digital consumption remained significantly lower. According to the study, a month without Facebook reduced anxiety and depressive symptoms by a quantum equivalent in terms of well-being to a gain of $30,000!

Sean Parker, formerly president of Facebook, had no hesitation in admitting that the firm's highest aim was to take advantage of 'the vulnerability in human psychology'. The whole point of all these social networks, from Facebook to TikTok, is to win this great 'battle for attention', whatever the psychological consequences for the targeted populations. Frances Haugen, a former Facebook employee, revealed in a document titled 'Facebook Files' that the company created by Mark Zuckerberg was fully aware of the psychological problems it was causing.

This Harvard-educated whistleblower, who spent two years at Facebook, sent the *Wall Street Journal* a series of compromising documents. Haugen explains that Facebook's research had perfectly grasped the fact that 'hateful, polarizing, divisive content' prompted more engagement, and that the company knowingly made use of this. It also showed that Facebook executives were perfectly aware of the psychological disorders created by its subsidiary Instagram among under-thirteen-year-old girls uncomfortable with their bodies. But that didn't stop the firm from targeting exactly this population.

Social networks whip up competition to attract attention and feed a constant effort at self-distinction, through provocation, exaggeration, venting and even the pleasure of saying the unspeakable and showing the unrepresentable. This extremist one-upmanship induces powerful emotional responses, particularly anger and indignation, which are immediately expressed through likes and retweets, and which technology automatically amplifies, without mediation, distance or delay.

Just fuck?

Eva Illouz has analysed how Tinder is transforming love lives.[5] Tinder is a way of finding a partner without having to 'waste' time wooing each other, and without having to deal emotionally with the consequences of a sexual relationship. The 'one-night stand' is certainly nothing new in human history. What is new is the place it now occupies in the imagination of teenagers. In the past, 'sexual intercourse marked the end of the romantic courtship; today, it is the beginning of a story with an uncertain future'. As one woman interviewed by Eva Illouz put it, sex in the digital age removes the hassle of having to 'manage the other person's emotional baggage'. Casual sex creates a psychological state in which both partners believe they are in complete control, with no dependence on others. It's just about the opposite of what a loving relationship involves. The Tinder version of love creates an existential void that you have to fill by meeting new people, in a constant cycle that is exactly representative of the addictive behaviours driven by today's society. Industrial society operates on a just-in-time basis. Tinder-style love lives are becoming a matter of 'just fuck'. By radically distinguishing between sex and the feeling of love, digital sexuality makes us lose

---

[5] Eva Illouz, *La Fin de l'amour*, Paris: Le Seuil, 2020.

the ability to recognize the other person as a whole – indeed, as a person – in a relationship where each of us expects the person we love to open the doors to a life that is yet to be invented.

8

The Environmental Crisis

A congested planet

In addition to being slaves to our digital devices, we are living under a dark shadow that is now hanging over all nations: climate change. This is the effect of industry's dependence on fossil fuels, from coal to oil. Up until the eighteenth century, humanity had depended on the sun and, to a lesser extent, water and wind as sources of energy. Everything changed with the Industrial Revolution. The combustion of fossil fuels and deforestation considerably increased the concentration of CO_2. Greenhouse gases (of which CO_2 is the main culprit) have one remarkable property: they allow the ultraviolet (short-frequency) rays emitted by the sun to pass through the atmosphere and warm the Earth. But they block the long-frequency infrared rays that the Earth itself emits. So, they let the sun's rays in, but trap the resulting heat, like in a greenhouse. Since 1850, the average temperature has risen by 0.8°C. Even if we were to completely stop emitting CO_2 today, the temperature would continue to rise by 0.5°C, because the warming of the oceans happens over time.

CO_2 fills the atmosphere in the same way that water fills a bathtub. It doesn't matter whether it was emitted a century ago or ten days ago: what matters for the climate is the overall quantity that has built up over time. Forests and oceans capture a (small) part of what is emitted but, despite this leakage, the climate bathtub is irresistibly filling up. There comes a time when it overflows. According to IPCC estimates, 85 per cent of our carbon budget has already been used up. To give you an idea of just how fast it is filling up, we have emitted almost as much CO_2 since 1990 (40 per cent of the total) as we did between 1850 and 1989. In April 2022, the IPCC reported that the bathtub would overflow if the trend was not reversed before 2025. For, by then, we would be irrevocably committed to global warming of more than 1.5°C. Rising temperatures are already responsible for more intense heat waves every summer, more forest fires, more rainfall and rising sea levels.

Scientists believe that an increase of 1.5°C above pre-industrial levels is the limit that must not be crossed. Beyond that threshold, all kinds of disruption are possible. Some of them are already visible: rising sea levels, the transmission of diseases to regions such as the African high plateaux that had earlier been protected from them by the temperate climate, increased desertification, increasing scarcity of available water, and also the opposite threat of melting glaciers and new floods. Other events may take place that, though remaining unlikely, will have unforeseeable consequences if they do occur. For instance, if the Gulf Stream were to change direction, Europe will be struck by a new Ice

Age. Complex extra factors will also add to future CO_2 emissions. When the tundra ice thaws, it is possible that further quantities of CO_2 will be released. The warming of the oceans could also release CO_2 and methane that are currently trapped in the seas. Another example is the cryosphere, the name given to the ice on the surface of land and oceans. If the Greenland ice cap were to melt, this would cause a five-metre rise in sea levels.

Collapse

Human societies have a surprisingly poor capacity to imagine themselves in their own future. This is surely cause for concern in today's context. Faced with the prospect of paying high costs in the here and now for the sake of some poorly defined long-term objective, it's hard to take collective action. Humanity's past is littered with examples of 'broken histories', of civilizations that have had to take a step back, like Europe after the fall of the Roman Empire, or the first industrial capitalism when it realized what a disaster this meant for the physical and moral condition of the workers.

The standard work for understanding the logic of ecological crises – a combination of denial and a stunned inability to act – is Jared Diamond's *Collapse*.[1] The example of Easter Island is one of the most striking in his narrative. The island was blanketed with palm trees, which enabled its inhabitants to build boats to fish for dolphins and porpoises. Tree trunks were also used to build sledges for transporting and erecting the famous

[1] Jared Diamond, *Collapse: How Societies Choose to Fail or Succeed*, London: Penguin, 2005.

statues of gigantic figures looking up to the sky. The last palm tree was felled in 1400. According to Diamond, the rivalry between tribes prevented a 'rational' collective management of the common asset, palm wood. None of the tribes wanted to drop out of the scramble to cut down the trees, fearing that this might strengthen their competitors.

Game of Thrones is a marvellous new take on this apocalyptic risk. It has been one of the most successful of the new epic series. 'Winter is coming' is the now cult phrase that runs through the various episodes. The coming winter is not just another season, but a mini-Ice Age. The series magnificently embodies the climatic threat, making it real, so to speak, by awakening an army of undead, the White Walkers, from the far north, ready to invade the kingdom. As in the true story of Easter Island, the princes' rivalry over the throne makes them totally insensitive to the risk posed by the White Walkers. The realization comes thanks to the hero, Jon Snow, a sort of Christ reincarnate. He is imagined to be a bastard, when in fact he is the true heir to the throne. Snow saves the kingdom from disaster by giving of himself and his love – earning no reward from his peers for this other than the right to go into exile in the far north. In the final scene, which brings eight years of waiting to a close for the audience, we understand that in this exile he will nevertheless find the true freedom of someone who has fulfilled his mission.

Collapsology

The best-selling book *How Everything Can Collapse: A Manual for our Times* has come to represent a manifesto for collapsology, the science of collapse.[2] The authors drew on and updated the prophetic analysis formulated by a team at MIT in 1972, known as the Meadows Report, which demonstrated that industrial society was about to come up against the world's finite limits. Quickly translated into various languages, this report announced that vast difficulties in terms of accessing non-renewable resources would force industrial societies to make a sharp and rapid course correction. The MIT book offered an extensive analysis of the growing footprint of human activities on soils, water and forests. Today, it resonates as a striking forewarning of the problems that now face the world. It owes much of its success to the fact that it also heralded the foreseeable end of fossil fuels, in retrospect making it the harbinger of the oil crisis.

Yet, as we are now discovering, the problem does not lie in the scarcity of fossil fuels. In fact, the problem is quite the opposite: it's that they are so abundant! The excess of fossil fuels is the factor that is endangering the Earth's ecosystem. If we decided to use up all our oil reserves, we would emit 20,000 gigatonnes of CO_2 – twenty-five times more than our carbon budget. However, the central message of the Meadows Report remains as relevant as ever to all the other issues it addresses.

Even assuming that governments actually implement the measures they have announced, global warming could reach 2.8°C before the end of the century. In its April 2022 report, the IPCC listed the measures that

[2] Pablo Servigne and Raphaël Stevens, *How Everything Can Collapse: A Manual for our Times*, Cambridge: Polity, 2020.

need to be taken to avoid such a disaster. We urgently need to transform our energy model and switch to renewable energies. We need to radically change our eating habits and give much more room to consuming plant-based food, change our transport habits by giving priority to rail, and rethink the way we organize our space. The transition will also, perhaps most importantly, require an in-depth examination of global inequalities. The richest 10 per cent alone emit 40 per cent of global CO_2, two-thirds of which comes from rich countries. The poorest 50 per cent emit just 13 per cent of the total. The average Afghan, for example, emits one tonne per year, while a French person emits almost ten times that amount (including emissions produced on their account in other countries).

The ecological class

Climate is not a new religion, or even an ersatz religion in our secularized world. It does not escape the usual categories of political life. When we look at voter preferences, we see a variety of opinions in this area that chimes closely with their overall political position. Voters on the left are in favour of combating global warming, whereas this is much less true of voters on the right. In France, voters for Marine Le Pen's National Rally are the least interested. Anyone counting on unanimous enthusiasm in favour of climate action is in for disappointment. For most people, the environment is important, but no more so than the health system or paying the bills. Awareness of the climate catastrophe has certainly increased. Polls show that three-quarters of French people now believe that global warming is a serious threat and that it is the consequence of human actions. But there is a broad range of opinion, between those who are prepared to bank everything on technical progress to find solutions and those who want to live in survivalist mode from now on. Such views differ so widely that it is difficult to feel any confidence about humans' collective capacity to agree on the actions that need to be taken.

The problem is greatly complicated by the fact that it's not just a question of reconciling who we are today with who we will be tomorrow: the reconciliation must take place here and now on a global scale. The poor countries that aspire to join the ranks of the rich countries have a hard time accepting that they should forsake cars and meat just because of the damage that has been caused by rich countries. Meanwhile, the French can convince themselves that this or that remedy – nuclear power, or more sober lifestyles – won't do much good anyway, if the Chinese, Americans or Indians don't go along too. We'd like to think that the climate problem offers human beings the key to a kind of universal awareness of their shared earthly dimensions. But that's a long way from being true.

If China were to adopt US consumption habits, by 2030 it could consume two-thirds of the world's cereal production such as it currently exists. If its paper consumption were to match US levels, it would consume 300 million tonnes: enough to swallow up all the world's forests! If the Chinese were one day to have three vehicles for every four inhabitants, following the American example, the infrastructure required in terms of road networks and car parks would exceed the area currently devoted to growing rice. As Lester Brown succinctly put it: the Western economic model is inapplicable to a population of 1.45 billion Chinese (as it is projected to be by 2030). Nor, of course, to India, whose population has already surpassed that of China.

As Bruno Latour and Nikolaj Schultz explain in their book, we ought to accept the idea that ecology does deeply divide society.[3] We need, they argue, to create a new 'class front' that includes all those who see environmentalism as an essential dimension of their social identity. This could mean gardeners, scientists involved in geoscience, anthropologists, or investors who want to be sure of the social value of their investments fifty years from now. Or it could involve all the professionals who are prepared to stand up for the rationality of their work against a focus on performativity – for instance, health workers and teachers. They would act in the knowledge that, for the sake of ecology, they need a democratic confrontation with the rest of society.

It would be a mistake to counterpose thought and action: it's by doing things that we transform our imaginary. We have to start living differently, even if the initial gestures are symbolic, in order to learn how to invent a new world. We need to feel not just sadness about the old world that is crumbling, but joy for the possible future one. Smokers who give up cigarettes must feel that they are regaining the means to have a good life. Otherwise, they are simply mourning a lost happiness, and relapse is inevitable.

[3] Bruno Latour and Nikolaj Schultz, *On the Emergence of an Ecological Class: A Memo*, Cambridge: Polity, 2022.

9
Gross Domestic Happiness

Everyone's looking for happiness!

Everyone's looking for happiness, 'even those who hang themselves', as Blaise Pascal put it. The modern world can best be defined by the idea that happiness on Earth is humanity's goal. Looking back over the centuries, it seems that progress has been made. In yesteryear, in Thomas Hobbes's famous phrase, life was 'nasty, brutish and short'. Today, in the rich countries at least, life is long and prosperous, and democracy and freedom of opinion reign. But that's not how people think. For most of them, life seems barely any less tough than it used to be. Around 15 per cent of Americans under the age of thirty-five have experienced a major depressive episode. In France, the consumption of psychotropic drugs has multiplied sixfold over the past few decades. In the United States, indicators of well-being are down by almost 30 per cent on the levels reached in the 1950s. Survey after survey come up with the same result: happiness is regressing or stagnating in wealthy societies, in France as elsewhere.

How can we understand the paradox of a society that sets itself a goal that it always misses? Why does happiness seem harder to achieve today than in the past, despite the much greater material wealth of developed countries? One answer immediately springs to mind: humans cannot be happy because they get used to everything. The progress we make, whatever it may be, soon becomes the norm. There is always a blank page to imagine new standards of happiness. But since a human being never foresees this adjustment of their expectations, their dreams remain inexhaustible. This is not necessarily discouraging. It's also a trait that allows us to keep our faith in a better future intact – a form of eternal youth. But it also demands that we understand how this process works.

Richard Easterlin

In 1974, the economist Richard Easterlin published a study that caused a stir. It drew economists' attention to this point, which is essential for understanding the determinants of well-being.[1] By tracking responses to the question 'Are you happy?' over thirty years, he showed that there was no shift over time even despite a tremendous increase in wealth over the period concerned. This is what economists went on to call the Easterlin paradox. The French were incomparably

---

[1] Richard A. Easterlin, 'Does Economic Growth Improve the Human Lot?' in David and Melvin W. Reder (eds.), *Nations and Households in Economic Growth: Essays in Honor of Moses Abramovitz*, New York: Academic Press, 1974.

richer in 1975 than in 1945, but they were no happier. Why?

Let's start with the basic problem: what is happiness? In answering this question, the survey respondents always put their financial situation first, followed by their family and health. In 1960, 65 per cent of Americans surveyed cited their financial well-being, 48 per cent health and 47 per cent family. Thirty years later, the figures had hardly changed. Making a good living was mentioned by 75 per cent of the Americans questioned, 50 per cent of them referred to success in their family life; health dropped down the scale a little, with one-third citing it as a main factor. War, freedom and equality were now mentioned much less often: these issues were brought up by fewer than one in ten. The figures are remarkably stable across different countries and political systems. In Cuba in 1960, for example, the corresponding figures were 73, 52 and 47 per cent; in Yugoslavia during the same period, the responses were 83, 60 and 40 per cent, respectively.

If wealth is such an important factor in our happiness, how come a society that is getting richer is apparently failing to make its members any happier? The simplest explanation is the following: consumption is like a drug. I can no longer do without things that ten years ago I didn't even know existed. Once you've got access to mobile phones and the Internet, they become indispensable. Consumption creates dependency. The pleasure that it offers is only fleeting, but we feel immense despair when we are denied it. These hunches are corroborated by many recent studies. Works by researchers like Daniel Kahneman and Amos Tversky or Andrew Clark show that rising incomes make people happy, but that the satisfaction derived from boosting your income quickly evaporates. According to these studies, 60 per cent of this satisfaction will have disappeared after just two years. Analyses of voter behaviour are even more daunting. When they go to the polls, voters only seem to take into account the economic situation over the previous six months.

Yet, this initial explanation is not a comprehensive answer to the question. Because in any given society, the rich are happier. If the addiction to getting richer were the only cause, the rich would be just as glum as the poor. But 90 per cent of richer people say they are very or fairly happy, while only 65 per cent of the poorest say they are. People who are financially well-off are still mostly very happy. If it were all just a question of being addicted to wealth, then this wouldn't be the case.

Brother-in-law syndrome

The explanation for this result, which will surprise no one, lies in a simple and eternal phenomenon: envy. We enjoy being more successful than others. Marx had already made this observation: 'A house may be large or small; as long as the neighbouring houses are likewise small, it satisfies all social requirement for a residence. But let there arise next to the little house a palace, and the little house shrinks to a hut.'[2] Everyone tries to outdo their colleagues or friends, those who form the 'reference group' with whom they compare themselves. As a nineteenth-century comedian put it:

[2] Karl Marx, *Wage Labour and Capital*, Ch. 6, text from Marxists Internet Archive.

'Happiness is earning more dollars than your brother-in-law.' Experimental studies show that people playing a game are prepared to lose part of their own winnings in order to reduce the winnings of other participants. Andrew Clark has shown that there is sometimes even a negative correlation between job satisfaction and a spouse's salary. In US families, a surprising observation has been made: a woman is more likely to work if her sister's husband earns more than her own husband. She has to compensate for the feeling that she is losing out as compared to her sister.

People can both be genuinely saddened by the misfortune of others and immediately envious of those who are more successful than they are. In a laboratory experiment in which they were asked about their preferences, students at one US university replied that they would prefer to earn $50,000 if their fellow students earned $25,000, rather than $100,000 if the others earned $200,000. The results of this experiment can be seen in real life.

All in all, through envy or dreams, each person measures their aspirations against those of some reference group. This may be a large group at the start of their lives (cousins, classmates, etc.) But, as time goes by, the reference group is usually reduced to the few close friends who share their social destiny. When the careers of two friends diverge, it becomes hard to do joint activities. What holidays and restaurants best suits both of them, when one is rich and the other poor? Divergences in our material fates will also fragment the world of emotional life.

However, human rivalry does not apply in all areas. When it comes to leisure, for example, it vanishes. The same American students were asked to choose between two options: (1) you have two weeks' holiday and your colleagues only one, or (2) you have four weeks' holiday and the others eight; they all chose the second option: to go on holiday for four weeks. There is no mimetic behaviour, in this case. The rivalry only concerns the visible features of social success. The unseen happiness of others, such as them having more free time, does not harshen this competition.

However you assess these results, one simple and stark conclusion remains: growth gives everyone hope, however fleeting it might be, of rising above their circumstances, catching up with others and exceeding their expectations. *Improving* one's situation is what makes a society happy. Modern societies are hungry for *growth* rather than wealth. It's better to live in a poor country that's getting richer (fast) than in an (already) rich country that's stagnating. The French loved the Trente Glorieuses because everything was new. But, at the end of the day, there's always a blank page of happiness yet to be conquered. However fast economic development may be at a given moment, a society is inevitably overtaken by frustration when growth is slow.

Epicurean happiness

In 1998, the king of Bhutan declared that his country's goal was to achieve the world's highest level of Gross National Happiness. But in 1999, he made a fatal mistake: he lifted the ban on owning a television. Rupert Murdoch immediately provided forty-six channels through his Star TV network. As a result, the kingdom's inhabitants saw the usual batch of sex, violence, advertising, and romance that people in rich countries were watching. The results were not long in coming. Divorces, crime, and drug use all spiked.

The digital revolution has since swept away the reign of television, but the result is the same. Too much time spent in front of screens leads people to neglect their friends, families and community life. The reign of the impulsive wins out over the realm of deeper thinking. Consumption becomes an addiction, like drugs. Economists have analysed addiction as a matter of 'time-inconsistent preferences'. I'd like to stop drinking, but I just can't. I'd like to read a book rather than watch a TV series, but I can't manage to do that either. To use the language of psychoanalysts, the human being is torn between the 'id', which seeks instant gratification, and the 'superego', which pushes for delayed gratification that raises them above themselves. Psychologists have even identified two regions of the brain: the limbic system for instant gratification, and the lateral pre-frontal cortex (the calculating part of the brain) for delayed gratification. Two quite distinct parts of our being do battle for our attention.

Economists have long scoffed at the distinction between vulgar pleasures and those that elevate the soul. Those who understand the beauty of an artwork are surely happier than others. The effort that it takes to understand the artistic power of an opera is repaid through greater happiness, like making an investment. But this does not create a qualitative difference between opera and TV, only a difference of degree. One expert in the science of happiness, Richard Layard, readily admits that variables such as purpose in life, and positive relationships with others – and with oneself – count for a great deal.

But why should we set them against the pursuit of other, more trivial satisfactions: having a good car or a nice flat? Going to the funfair can be just as satisfying as going to church; indeed, the same person can do both and calibrate the time required for each. It's all a question of getting the right dose. Just like a sovereign wielding all the levers of power, *Homo economicus* freely chooses, according to this model, both the good and the bad, the time spent working and the hours spent sleeping in.

But who can believe in such a rational schema? Far from managing his affects according to some diligently prepared formula, each human being is a composite of diverse personalities that coexist more or less harmoniously. You might be on your way to an appointment vital for your career, but you still jump into the water to save a drowning passer-by. There's no calculation at work here. Under the influence of your emotions, you pass from one condition to another.

The desire to live up to some ideal comes up against the desire for instant gratification that distances us from this ideal. How can we teach them to coexist? The famous example of Ulysses and the sirens provides an illustration of possible approaches. For Jon Elster, who wrote a famous commentary on this passage from *The Odyssey*, what Odysseus needs to do is 'rationally manage his irrationality'. I know what I am tempted to do: give in to the sirens' song. I'll manage these temptations up front by tying to a mast the person I don't want to become. If I'm on a diet to lose weight, I'll avoid going past a bakery. If I need to save up for old age, I'll take out an illiquid investment to avoid spending it. I'm fighting against the person whom I might become. The *Homo economicus* within me is struggling. He lacks what we might simply call wisdom.

Finding your place

Epicurus – whose disciples aspirants to happiness often believe themselves to be – is in line with the modern idea, expounded by Jeremy Bentham in the eighteenth century, that we should both seek pleasure and avoid pain. But Epicurus takes great care to distinguish between 'kinetic' pleasures, linked to the satisfaction of a need, and thus mixed with pain, and pure, 'static' pleasures, which presuppose that desires have been satisfied. In the *Gorgias*, Plato is more radical. In his view, the pursuit of happiness suffers from a fundamental contradiction: happiness needs desire, while desire excludes happiness. For Plato, happiness, if it is to be called that, is the reward of 'a good life', not its goal. A good life (*eudaino-mia*) means finding one's place in the human world, like one star revolving in harmony around another. Aristotle prudently concludes that since the specificity of man is reason and virtue, 'the lovers of what is noble find pleasant the things that are by nature pleasant; and virtuous actions are such, so that these are pleasant for such men as well as in their own nature. Their life, therefore, has no further need of pleasure as a sort of adventitious charm, but has its pleasure in itself.'[3]

Taking his cue from Epicurus, the economist Bruno Frey has proposed a classification that is very

---

[3] Aristotle, *Nicomachean Ethics*, Book I/8, trans. W.D. Ross.

useful for understanding the mechanisms at work when people compare themselves to others. He suggests a distinction between 'extrinsic' and 'intrinsic' goods. The first group concerns status and wealth: these are the outward signs of social success, the social assets we accumulate over time, which mark the place that each of us has in society. Intrinsic experiences are linked to having the affection of others ('relatedness'), love, the feeling of having a purpose in life. These are 'flow' experiences, which slide along with the time that passes. Extrinsic goods sharpen social rivalries, whereas intrinsic goods silently increase well-being.

Unless you are either a saint or a socialite, you certainly need both of these be happy (Schopenhauer said: unless you are 'stoic or Machiavellian'). But the problem is that we find it hard to understand our own emotions, and systematically underestimate the benefits of intrinsic goods. Many people dream of a beautiful home, and choose to move away from the city centre to find better value for money. But they ignore the psychological cost of commuting, and often end up regretting their choices, even if they do not want to admit it.

The lessons of life

Why is it so hard to understand what's good for us? Daniel Kahneman, a trained psychologist, has grappled with this question. He shows that we tend to remember only two moments: the most intense one and the last one. When I go on holiday, I remember the most exciting day, and the goodbyes on the train station platform. Everything else fades away in the blur of life passing by. This 'peak–end' model makes people forget the moments in between. In so doing, when people imagine themselves in the future, they also tend to ignore the 'duration' of life. They picture themselves in experiences with a 'strong peak', to the detriment of others with a 'strong flow'. The memory struggles to retain the silent emotions of ordinary days. Proust's genius in *In Search of Lost Time* is to show the fight we have against our own selves in order to overcome our usual propensity to remember only the most striking moments. 'Lost time' has the double meaning of past time that we think that we've forgotten, and the time that we consider wasted on futile questions, which were in fact the most important thing of all.

As we grow older, however, it is possible that a newly acquired wisdom will make us understand what's good for us. Indeed, there is a surprising relationship between happiness and age. It resembles a U-shape: young people and senior citizens are (much) happier than middle-age adults. From the age of twenty-five to fifty, happiness steadily declines, then rises again. At seventy, we rediscover the happiness of a young person aged thirty. At the age of eighty, we've regained (on average) the joy we had when we were eighteen. How can we understand this surprising finding? Does being close to death not make us lose hope? Economists are, doubtless, hardly in the best position to answer this question. However, the distinction offered by Bruno Frey helps us to grasp what might be at stake. Old age frees us from a burden – the weight of accumulating useless goods – and gives intrinsic goods their proper place back. Old age opens us up to the simple pleasure of time passing. In his book *Testaments Betrayed*, Milan Kundera marvelled at Beethoven's work 'towards the end of his life'. It was then that this master

composed sonatas that broke with the codes of traditional composing styles. For Kundera, this was the work
of a genius freed from the burden of having to be a
genius, and of having to please others.

Living happily is possible

Armed with these lessons, Bruno Frey takes up the
challenge – not without some panache – of offering
lessons in life that can be understood as lessons in pru-
dence. There is always an element of irony in explaining
what to do in this area. Still, these lessons have the great
merit of shedding light on what efforts need to be made
in order to resist the often adverse currents of social life.
Here are his ten tips (rather than commandments):

1. Don't worry about not being a genius, because
   geniuses are no happier than anyone else. One of
   the secrets of happiness can be summed up quite
   simply: compare yourself with those who have less
   than you. On average, bronze medallists are happier than silver medallists (this has been statistically
   confirmed). Silver medallists compare themselves to
   gold medallists. Bronze medallists compare themselves to those who have nothing.
2. Earn money, but don't make this into an illness.
   A pay rise makes you happy – but only for a few
   months. In less than a year, 40 per cent of the pleasure has already evaporated, and you have to earn
   even more to find satisfaction.
3. Age gracefully. Provided you're in good health,
   ageing doesn't affect your happiness. On the contrary, like Beethoven, you can find the pleasure, late

in life, of a new creativity, freed from the constraint of producing a 'great work'.

4. Don't compare yourself to others when it comes to beauty. Standards are unrealistic. The pressure supermodels put on your psyche creates unnecessary frustration.

5. 'Believe' in something: God, social justice or the beauty of nature; you need a sense of the 'meaning of life' in order to be happy and escape from self-obsession.

6. Help others: altruism takes you away from being concerned just with yourself, and that feels good, for the same reasons.

7. Control your desires. New 'aspirations' always outstrip 'achievements', however lofty the latter may be.

8. Hold on to your friends: they are the dearest assets, even if they are the least visible ones.

9. Live as a couple, because solitude does you no good.

10. Accept what you are and deal rationally with your weaknesses. If you are a procrastinator, understand this and set yourself some rules. But conversely, if you are mentally rigid, then force yourself to transgress them.

One great merit of this list is that it indirectly highlights the fact that society pushes each of us to follow almost the exact opposite of these precepts in our daily lives. For society pushes us to compare ourselves to Steve Jobs, athletes and supermodels – in short, to encourage us to make ourselves the source of our own unhappiness. But, as anyone can experience for themselves, there is nothing inevitable in this respect.

Conclusion

Human history is littered with problems that humans did not understand. When they conquered the planet, driven by uncontrollable demographic pressure, the apocalypse was already deemed 'inevitable'. Friday, 13 November 2026 was identified as the day of reckoning, the day when there would be too many human beings. The whole Earth might then look like the societies devastated by environmental crises that turned out to be impossible to control: ancient Mesopotamia, Easter Island, the Mayans and the Vikings. But humanity averted the predicted disaster thanks to an upheaval that nobody had anticipated at the time: the demographic transition, which drastically reduced the female fertility rate. Today, we need a similar scale of transition regarding the material civilization we have now entered into. Will we succeed?

Malthus's law is no longer the driving force behind human societies. It has been replaced by another, Easterlin's paradox – a force that humanity again has a hard time understanding, and whose effects are likewise extreme. Like a hiker who never reaches the horizon, the modern human wants always to become richer, without understanding that this wealth, once attained, will become the normal condition from which they will want to rise up again. Humans are starving for material wealth, just as they used to hunger for calories in agrarian societies, without this desire ever being sated.

Why do human beings constantly want to tear themselves away from themselves? It's an impenetrable question that psychoanalysts, anthropologists and economists have tried to answer, each in their own way. Still, the essence of the problem can be summed up in one simple line: human desire adapts to the circumstances of history, but in a way that is always just as stubborn. It doesn't really matter on what level this desire is expressed, as long as it allows humans to sublimate themselves in some job, some work, and to play their part on the great stage of social life. In *The Accursed Share*, Georges Bataille offers a magnificent and baroque list of these possibilities. The Aztecs, for example, built immense pyramids on top of which they immolated human beings. 'Their world view is singularly and diametrically opposed to the activity-oriented perspective that we have', says Bataille, 'They were just as concerned about sacrificing as we are about working.'[1] The Native Americans' 'potlatch' is another example of a situation where the solemn gift of riches, offered by a chief to his rival, aims to humiliate him, to challenge him, to force him to reciprocate. The Tibetans give all their surplus to the monasteries, the only accepted form

[1] Georges Bataille, *The Accursed Share: An Essay on General Economy*, vol. 1, trans. Robert Hurley, New York: Zone Books, 1988, p. 46.

of earthly wealth, until the whole of society is exhausted by toil. Everywhere, sacrifices, festivals and wars absorb the excess energy of a society, and each time in a unique way.

The modern world reserves this exuberance for material wealth. However, a new turn has by now become essential – one that will take us, like the demographic transition, from quantity to quality. Faced with this immense challenge, *Homo economicus* is a poor prophet indeed. In trying to overcome the obstacles that stand in the way of enrichment, he is driving out his competitors, the *Homo ethicus* and the *Homo empathicus*, these other parts of the human being that aspire to cooperation and reciprocity. But in triumphing over its rivals, he has metamorphized into a *Homo numericus* obsessed with consumption and his own ego, and is now condemned to live in an unfeeling world that is increasingly devoid of ideals.

Admittedly, human beings have a powerful capacity for adaptation. Our obsession with comparing ourselves with others allows us to go anywhere, as long as others go there too. However, it is an anthropological illusion to think that competition will be enough to put the world in order. This would come at a high cost, if it were not offset by other, compensatory passions. In the balance between competition and cooperation, we need to breathe new life into the second, by re-enchanting work, re-examining the boundaries between what is free and what has to be paid for, and re-inventing international cooperation.

It's up to us now to rethink our idea of a world in harmony with itself, one that makes us feel 'a foretaste of happiness and peace'.

Afterword

by Michel Cohen

My brother Daniel was excited by the idea of writing a comic strip. He wanted to do this so that he could share with as many people as possible, of all ages, his educational and didactic overview of the history of the economy and his intellectual journey over the past fifty years.

We were talking about this project in Corsica by the sea during our last summer together in August 2022, a year before this terrible illness took him away from us. I can still see the sparkle in his eyes, the expression on his face and the characteristic movement of his arms as the ideas swirled around in his head.

When I first read the manuscript that you have just discovered, I was struck by the brilliant panoramic vision offered by his text. I felt as if I were looking at his 'brief history of the economy', as always anchored in a rigorous scholarly approach, and his own interpretation of the evolution of the world economy.

My brother loved cinema – ever since he was given a 16mm camera at the age of thirteen. As I read this work in one sitting, I had the impression that I was watching the thread of his thoughts and reflections over the past fifty years being narrated by him as if in a film.

So, together with his publisher – and accomplice – at Albin Michel, Alexandre, and his good friend Laury, we thought that this text deserved to be published as is, in its raw version, as a series of rushes put end to end, just as my brother had imagined it. And ultimately produced.

After discussing it with his wife Martine and his daughters Pauline and Clara, we were all convinced that my brother would have liked this text to be published as it stood, after his death, even if it wasn't yet perfect, at least according to his standards.

We would thus like to extend our warmest thanks to his French publisher for agreeing to publish Daniel's last posthumous text as he wrote it. An illustrated version, which will find snippets of inspiration in this rich text, will soon follow in the form of a comic strip, as he had originally intended.

We would also like to thank Esther Duflo, who agreed to write a preface to this book and chair the jury that will award the Daniel Cohen Chair in Economics and the Daniel Cohen Prize in Economics, which will receive all the royalties from the collectively written book, *Daniel Cohen, l'économiste qui voulait changer le monde* (*Daniel Cohen, The Economist Who Wanted to Change the World*).

Finally, we hope that throughout these pages you have shared the same pleasure and interest as we did, letting yourself be carried away by the film of his thoughts. We hope you followed the flame that Daniel left to us, to arrive at the 'foretaste of happiness and peace'.